More Memo
of Norfolk

The Author   (Photo: *Trevor Ranger*)

More Memories of Norfolk

by

Robert Bagshaw

By the Same Author:

Poppies to Paston
Toothy Goes to War
Norfolk Remembered

ISBN   Hardback: 0 900616 41 5
        Paperback: 0 900616 42 3

        Printed and published by
        Geo. R. Reeve Ltd., Damgate, Wymondham, Norfolk

Contents

Foreword 9

1 A Fine City? 11

2 Gentlemen of the Press 20

3 Café Royal and Mugs' Hall 30

4 Norwich Hill 40

5 Hidden Places 50

6 Forgotten Heroes 63

7 The T.D.L. 74

8 Mysterious Norfolk 81

9 The Age of the Train 89

10 The Hustings 102

11 The Fun of the Fair 110

12 Beachmen of Yarmouth and Gorleston 122

13 Wymondham — Friday Sale and Whit Thursday Sports . 132

14 North Walsham — The Family Business 143

15 What's in a Name? 157

16 Simple Folk 165

Acknowledgements 175

Illustrations

The Author . . . . Frontispiece

Castle Gardens, Norwich 14

Chapelfield Gardens, Norwich 14

Victoria Station, formerly Ranelagh Gardens 17

Number 57, London Street, Norwich, 1899 21

The Press Office under construction, 1900 22

Gentlemen of the Press 26

The Café Royal, Norwich 31

London Street, Norwich, 1932 33

Kingswood House, otherwise 'Mugs' Hall' 37

Norwich Cattle Market 41

Spelman's Horse Sale, 1912 45

Hay Hill as George Green knew it 47

Lambert's Oriental Café 51

Norwich Canaries in their Nest 54, 57

The Rosary Cemetery 59-61

Norwich welcomes Harry Daniels V.C., 1915 66

The City's reception for Sidney Day V.C., 1917 72

The Theatre de Luxe 75, 78, 79

The Lobster Coach on its run from Norwich to Cromer 90

Railway fitting shops and houses, Melton Constable 93

Railway staff and shunting horses, Wymondham 97

Bass Brewery employees arriving at Yarmouth, 1909 100

Boys of the Paston School leaving North Walsham, 1935 . . 100

Employees of the Briton Brush Company
  leaving Wymondham 101

Election mayhem at Ludham and Stalham, 1895 107

North Walsham Market Place 108

Children's Corner at Tombland Fair, 1910 111

The Trinity Outing from Stalham to Eccles 115

Showmen and their ladies, Woolpit Fair, 1897 116

Showmen and their horses, early 1900s 117

Walter and Violet Underwood 120

George Holmes' stall on Yarmouth beach 123

Goat carts await their young passengers 124

The Concert Ring, Great Yarmouth 124

Chappell's Promenade Concert 126

Gorleston Pier 128

William Adams, Gorleston's 'human fish' 130

Fairland Street, Wymondham 133

Wymondham's Whit Thursday Sports 137, 140

Jesse Harvey, the Wymondham Bellman 138

Mr. Grey and his North Walsham shop 144

Arthur Griffin of North Walsham 146

George Fuller with St. John Ambulance colleagues 149

Fred Randell and his two shops 150, 151

Edward Le Grice propagating his roses 153

The princesses' house that Bob Farman thatched 155

Cromer Lifeboat *Louisa Heartwell* and her crew 158

'Belcher' Johnson 162

'Squinter' West 162

'Latter-day' Cox 163

'Old Pegg' 163

The Pettingale brothers of Castle Rising 171

Four Norfolk Veterans 172

Oh, there are Voices of the Past,
Links of a broken chain,
Wings that can bear me back to times
Which cannot come again —
Yet God forbid that I should lose
The echoes that remain!

(Lines written by Adelaide Ann Procter and inscribed on the back of the staircase in Willy Lott's Cottage at Flatford Mill).

FOREWORD

by Ben Burgess M.B.E.

Surely there was never a time when the columns of local book reviews and the shelves of bookshops were so burdened by reminiscences, biographies and autobiographies about Norfolk rural life of the not so distant past. Probably because I am an old cynic who has outlived his allotted span by another score or so, I now find myself beginning to cringe at the thought of approaching birthday or Christmas when the kindest and most well-meaning of my dear friends and relations decide which sort of reading I should most enjoy.

There can be little doubt that one of the easiest forms of authorship is to sit down and commit reminiscences to paper or tape recorder. I know because I am addicted to it. It requires no more research than occasionally to check a date or name a place. Unfortunately, most of the amateurs I call to mind seem to write about the doings of a generation older than their personal remembrance and bring these happenings forward into their own life and times! And they fall into the trap of adding imagined detail in their efforts to improve upon the original story.

By all means let anyone who has a story to tell make a permanent record of it, but let it be without embroidery or embellishment or even those "advantages" which Henry V warned his soldiers against when, in old age, they told the story of the coming battle. The truth is good enough. A departure from this principle only destroys the historical value of the record. That thought has brought me to my message in a foreword to this delightful miscellany compiled by Bob Bagshaw.

Like most readers, I judge and value any book by the authenticity of those parts which impinge onto my limited speciality. What impresses me is Bob's ability as a professional author to "switch on to the environment" surrounding his subjects. My personal test in this book is Bob's character interpretation of two men from extreme opposite ends of the Norfolk spectrum who deserve far more attention than has hitherto been given to them — the notorious bookmaker Dicky Dowson and the renowned rose grower Eddie Le Grice. The former was portrayed to me, when a child, as the very epitome of evil. This came not from my father or my uncle, both of whom had taken over farms abandoned by men who had become addicted to slow horses, hard liquor and Dicky's wiles. It came from the farm staff who had seen it all happening in slow motion before the final crash and my father's arrival. But nothing in life is all black. In point of fact, Dicky Dowson was the delightful character Bob has shown him to be in an age of drinking and gambling that we can hardly visualise a century later.

Eddie Le Grice was a strict Baptist who "lived up to his religion" as we used to say. He was my age and we went through the Paston School together. During the last two years we shared one of those lovely old oaken double desks (It would be a nice thought if Bob too had one twenty years later). In later life his dedication to his chosen work and his philosophy of life put me to shame. He did me good. Oh, how I used to enjoy our mutual journeys home from Liverpool Street on the 6.30. It was a ritual that I should make the motion to put a little claret from my half bottle into his glass, only to be answered by a whimsical smile and a slight shake of the hand — to the last we were still schoolboys.

What I have to thank Bob for, and I am sure other readers will share my gratitude, is an introduction to a number of hitherto little-known ordinary Norfolk people, few of whom ever hit the headlines for a single day. This prompts me to express my conviction that their modern contemporaries are still among us in the quiet places of our diverse and versatile county. If so, let us hope that somebody, at some time, will tell their story in the pages of such a book as this.

CHAPTER 1

A Fine City?

Back in the 1930s I proclaimed my belief that Norwich was the finest city in England. I was only eleven years old and had never been outside the boundary of my native county, but I knew there could be no other place in the kingdom to challenge my home city. There really is such a thing as love at first sight, and I willingly yielded to the charms of my loved one.

George Borrow had felt the same way about the place many years earlier when he was moved to write that oft-misquoted phrase, "A fine old city, truly, is that, view it from whatever side you will". He liked it best from the heights to the east, from which he gazed across the fair and fertile valley towards the "gray old castle . . . that cloud-encircled cathedral spire, and the thrice-twelve churches".

Norwich was a much bigger city by the time I met her, and she was a wonderland to inspire any young lad. I fell under her spell and, as one does with loved ones, I overlooked her faults. I gazed in fascination at the little yards off Ber Street and Magdalen Street, turning my mind towards their history rather than the plight of the poor people who lived there. I rode on the trams and delighted at each clank of the wheels and every flash of sparks from the overhead wires, forgetting (if I ever knew) the amount of demolition which had been necessary to enable them to plough their way through the city streets. But there was so much that was beautiful about the old city.

Norwich was not brightly-lit at the best of times and, as dusk fell — particularly on early closing day — the streets were virtually deserted. The cathedral and the castle were pools of darkness, past which the trams lumbered along like incredible time machines. But it was the very nature of the lighting which made it all so intriguing, for darkness can cover a multitude of faults. The feeble light of a street lamp would reveal an ancient, gnarled house or a little bow-fronted shop. Century after century was there, with a bit of lamplight suddenly accentuating an ancient gable, a Georgian doorway or a fat, bulging bay window. There was something almost Dickensian about Tombland and Princes Street, St. Giles' and St. Andrew's, so much so that, as one turned a corner, one might almost expect to bump into Edwin Drood or, perhaps, David Copperfield on his way to visit Peggotty at Yarmouth.

Then came the war and, in the years that followed, changes began to take place in the city. As time went by, so the pace of those changes became faster and I realised that all was not to my liking. My love for my native city was being tested to the full. Was Norwich, I asked myself, really the fine city I had always claimed her to be?

Quite recently, I expressed my doubts during the course of a visit to my hairdresser — a young man, I should emphasise, many years my junior.

"Fine city?" he said. "Of course Norwich is a fine city".

"Alright", I replied. "Tell me what it is about Norwich that makes you feel that way".

He answered with another question. "Have you", he said, "ever stood on the flyover at Grapes Hill at dusk and watched all the lights shining over the city? Lights in the shops and houses, lights in the office blocks, lights along the streets — you can even see the lights from car headlamps going along those streets — the whole place is alive".

I suddenly felt very old — or, at least, old-fashioned. My Norwich had gone. She had given way to a new Norwich — a city of the motor car, of speed and of 24-hour daylight. But I refused to break off my love affair with the place. I consoled myself with the thought that she was a City For All Centuries. And if I felt old, how fared George Borrow? It was the better part of two centuries since he knew Norwich, and it was not just a changed city — it was a different world.

At the dawning of the nineteenth century the population of Norwich numbered around 40,000, the majority of whom still lived within the city walls. A small proportion had scattered themselves in the little hamlets on the fringe of the city, and some of the more well-to-do members of society had established their mansions out there. Jeremiah Ives had built Town Close House and James Crowe had gone to Lakenham. John Gurney had transferred his household from Magdalen Street to Earlham, and Joseph Gurney was at The Lodge on Ipswich Road, where the City College now stands.

For the rest it was life within the flint walls, and there was plenty of room for everybody. The poor, of course, were herded together in their hovels, and they took up little enough space. Then there were the many hundreds of shopkeepers who lived above their premises. For the rest, there were vast areas of garden ground. It is difficult nowadays to imagine a house in Magdalen Street with a garden extending to four acres. Such, however, was the case with Lord Bradford's home, later to become the property of the Blind Institution. Then there was Matthew Brettingham's garden near St. Augustine's Gates. I am not aware of its actual acreage, but it was certainly large enough to enable him to set man-traps when intruders stole the oak stakes which supported his espalier trees. And there were the houses of Thomas Ivory's fine terrace in Surrey Street which, at that time, had gardens stretching back to the city wall with their thorn trees and tall elms.

In addition to the private gardens, there were Borrow's "thrice-twelve churches", and that meant an equal number of churchyards — and most of them were more extensive than they are nowadays. But, above all, the city boasted a wealth of public open spaces, many of which have been sacrificed to the demands of urban development. I have been told that a flight over Norwich at the present time reveals a large number of green pockets, but these are mostly sports grounds and school playing fields. Two centuries ago, such amenities, though not so neatly manicured, were larger and more numerous.

There was, for instance, the area around the Castle, much favoured by those citizens of fashion who were partial to a leisurely stroll, and described in 1792 by the writer of "A Norfolk Tale" in the following words:

> ... a terrace falls
> With gentle slope from those dread walls,
> Where beauty holds its daily court
> And all the Norwich belles resort.

There was also Chapel Field, though it must be admitted that it was not much used by ladies of a genteel nature because of the number of disorderly boys who gathered there, particularly on Sundays. Chapel Field has a history as rich as that of the city itself. Once the pasture of the great College of St. Mary in the Fields, it became the shooting butts at which the compulsory skills of archery were acquired during the Elizabethan age. When

Castle Gardens, "where all the Norwich belles resort".

Children at play by the old pagoda in Chapelfield Gardens.

fire-arms took the place of bows and arrows, it found itself being used for another purpose — it became the Plague Pit for the hurried mass burials of 1666. When the Plague finally wore itself out, Chapel Field became once again a public open space until early water engineers hit upon the idea of using it as a reservoir. Its shelving edges made it admirably suitable for such a purpose, and it remained so until the increasing demands of a growing city led to the beginnings of a more modern water supply system. Now, well-planted and handsome, Chapel Field has become a public park, an area of tranquillity on the edge of what used to be called the New City. And it is also a place of memories — memories of Elizabethan archers and of the men who, in 1914, drilled there before going off to fight on the Somme and at Passchendaele; memories, in my boyhood, of happy couples dancing to the strains of music from the bandstand and of children playing around the long-departed pagoda.

Norwich was also well-provided with Pleasure Gardens, where rich and poor alike could disport themselves at will. Many of these were associated with public houses, notably the Prussia Gardens at the King of Prussia on Ipswich Road and the Cellar House Gardens in Pockthorpe. Others were at the Greyhound in Ber Street, the Richmond Hill, further along at Ber Street Gate, and Harper's Gardens at the Cherry Tree in Southwell Street. But foremost among such gardens were those which numbered among their attractions a Pantheon, a Greek-style building in which concerts and other events could take place irrespective of weather conditions. The leading pair were Keymer's Vauxhall Gardens, situated between St. Faith's Lane and the river, and Quantrell's (later Coe's, then Neech's) Ranelagh Gardens outside St. Stephen's Gates. This latter had earlier been known simply as the Rural Gardens and eventually, when Queen Victoria came to the throne, it took her name, finally to become the site of Victoria railway station.

There was normally no fee for admission to the Gardens though, on such special occasions as Guild Days and during Assize Week, there was usually a charge of one shilling, with sixpence returned in the form of free liquor. At such times there would be concerts, firework displays and other entertainments. The people of Norwich followed the course of world events as closely as was possible and, following the Fall of the Bastille in Paris, William Quantrell advertised the Guild Day entertainments at his Rural Gardens in June 1790, closing with the following:

"The evening's amusements to conclude with 'Paris In An Uproar', or 'Assault On The Bastille' in which will be exhibited the Governor, Major, Guards, Emblems of Liberty etc taken on the spot. The Scenery and Machinery painted and executed by Mr. Ninham of this city".

Mr. Keymer, at the Vauxhall Gardens, was not to be outdone and, the following month, for Assize Week, he offered:

"The Triumph of Liberty, or Releasement From the Bastille — a picturesque view of the Bastille, the various instruments of torture, gloomy cells, skeletons, wretched victims chained in a variety of postures and liberated by the brave Henry Dubois".

And the scenery was painted by Mr. Keymer himself.

Rivalry was intense between the various Pleasure Gardens, and never more so than when local interest became caught up in the mysteries of flight. It is a sobering thought that, two centuries ago, men were actually flying over the city and the surrounding countryside. Admittedly, they were doing it in gas balloons rather than fixed-wing aircraft, but it was the first step towards conquest of the skies.

It all began in January 1784 when James Bunn constructed a balloon and had it floating in the Pantheon in his Public Spring Garden — the first known tethered flight in Norfolk. William Quantrell was quick to strike back and, the following month, a balloon five feet in diameter was launched from his Gardens, giving, in the words of the local newspaper, "the greatest pleasure to many hundred Ladies and Gentlemen who honoured the exhibition with their appearance and countenance". It took off in the direction of Wymondham and, after about seven or eight minutes, disappeared. Mr. Quantrell lost his balloon, but not before it had achieved the distinction of carrying out the county's first free flight. A fortnight later Mr. Bunn took his turn. Up went a balloon from his Gardens but, after about three minutes, it was hidden from sight by a dark cloud and never seen again.

Then, on March 15th 1784, they both had a go. At noon, before a crowd who had been invited to attend "at the trifling expense of sixpence each person, which will be returned in liquor", Mr. Quantrell released his balloon. It took off in a north-westerly direction and eventually landed seven miles away at Barford.

Victoria Station, the site of Mr. Quantrell's Ranelagh (later Victoria) Gardens.

By 5 p.m. the wind direction had changed slightly for, when Mr. Bunn released his balloon, it set off in a south-westerly direction and "afforded a most pleasing satisfaction to many thousands of spectators as it sped off as steady and rapid as an arrow from a bow". It fell at East Bradenham at 5-30, having covered 25 miles in half an hour.

It was on June 1st 1785 that the big breakthrough came — the first manned flight — and it was from Quantrell's Gardens. A certain James Deeker took off and, following a flight of ten miles eastwards, landed safely in a meadow at Sisland. Just to show it was no fluke, he later made another flight, landing twelve miles away at Topcroft.

Then, on to the scene came Major John Money, a larger-than-life character who, in today's parlance, "lived his life in the fast lane". He had previously flown with two passengers from Tottenham Court Road in London and, on July 23rd 1785, after first exhibiting his balloon in St. Andrew's Hall, he took off from Quantrell's Gardens before a crowd of several thousand people. The balloon floated steadily towards the coast, passing over Pakefield about an hour and a half later. At that point he decided to come down to earth by venting some of the gas, but it seems there was a fault in the mechanism. The balloon continued on its way, passed over the coast and eventually came down in the sea some twenty miles off Southwold. Fortunately for the Major, the balloon kept him afloat for five hours, when he was rescued by the revenue cutter *Argus* and brought ashore at Lowestoft.

To any lesser mortal the experience would have been a disaster, but John Money was made of sterner stuff. After all, he was a professional soldier who, when not answering his own country's call, was not above offering his services as a mercenary in such places as America and France. In 1792 he accepted an invitation to raise a legion for the French army, thereby acquiring the rank of General, and it was in Paris that he witnessed the tragic events leading up to the storming of the Bastille in the French Revolution. Then, sensing that war with England was inevitable, he resigned his commission, informing local newspapers of his action, lest he be accused of serving the enemy.

"When I engaged to serve these people", he said, "they had a King and Constitution; now they have neither − they are all mad".

He managed to obtain a passport to England for himself and his French valet. Then he discovered that the youthful Hudson Gurney from Earlham was stranded in France, unable to acquire one. Money immediately sacked his servant and brought young Gurney home in the man's livery.

John Money settled for the rank of Colonel and soon found his place in Norwich society. He had inherited an estate on the southern fringes of the city, calling it Crown Point after one of the battles in which he had been engaged in America. He developed the habit of organising an Annual Ball which was well-patronised by most of the leading citizens, and he was welcomed as a visitor by the Gurneys at Earlham. Elizabeth Gurney confided to her diary her sense of pleasure at meeting him, though she added a word of warning to herself. "It is better", she wrote, "to overlook such people as him who are so fascinating and not good characters". Did she, one wonders, regard him simply as *nouveau riche*, or could it have been anything to do with the fact that, though unmarried, he had two sons?

Colonel Money retained his interest in ballooning, but as a supporter rather than as a participant. He was at the Prussia Gardens on February 9th 1815 for the much-heralded ascent by Mr. Steward before an assembled crowd of several thousand onlookers. It was not the most successful of flights. The balloon rose slowly and tentatively, then skimmed dangerously over some

18

pine trees before coming to rest in the garden of a Mr. Halls, a mere 500 yards away in Lakenham. A crowd quickly gathered and, at first, tried to push it back into the air. Then there were threats and turmoil as the balloon became the object of popular fury, being torn into pieces and borne away by the crowd. Poor Mr. Steward suffered much physical abuse until Colonel Money arrived and, escaping into the colonel's carriage, he "was taken to his inn, where he bled and was put to bed".

Soon the ordinary citizens were calling for a chance to share in the joys of ballooning, and there was only one solution. A tethered gas balloon was installed on the old Cattle Market and, surrounded by a crowd numbering several thousands, many of them were taken aloft for an aerial view of their city. And it was George Borrow's Norwich that they looked down upon. Beneath them flowed the narrow river, crossed by an antique bridge and flanked on either side by rich meadows of the brightest green. There were the city's venerable houses, its numerous gardens, its thrice-twelve churches; there was the castle on its mound and the cathedral, with its spire encircled by a garrulous army of rooks. "No wonder", wrote Borrow, "that the children of that fine old city are proud of her and offer up prayers for her prosperity. I, myself, who was not born within her walls, offer up prayers for her prosperity, that want may never visit her cottages, nor vice her palaces".

George Borrow's love affair with Norwich began as he viewed the city, much smaller then than it is now, from the gipsy encampment on Mousehold Heath. My young friend's admiration, in complete contrast, arose as he stood on the Grapes Hill flyover and absorbed the vitality of the modern conurbation which Norwich has now become. My love, somewhere in between, was for the dimly-lit city of the thirties and the wonderment of riding on the top deck of a tram as it chuntered along past the architectural wonders of St. Giles' Street.

Perhaps, after all, the secret of a city's greatness is to be found not so much in its buildings but rather more in the hearts of its people.

CHAPTER 2

Gentlemen of the Press.

As a small boy I knew where my destiny lay — I would be a reporter on the *Eastern Daily Press*. After all, I had the pedigree for it. My father, my uncle and two brothers were all reporters and I, myself, had even been born in the room above the Press Office in Cromer. Then, at North Walsham, I had come under the guidance of a succession of teachers who awakened in me a feeling of wonderment at the richness and variety of the English language. Yes, I would be a reporter.

It was my mother who had other ideas. She was only too well aware that newspapermen lead strange lives and work unholy hours, and she already had three of them in the family, which was quite enough. So my destiny lay in tatters and I set off on the road to another profession.

But all was not lost. As a small boy, under my father's wing, I was introduced to the world of the Press at number 57, London Street in Norwich and it soon became my spiritual home. Over the years that followed, I met such a host of journalists of all kinds and developed lasting friendships with so many of them that, though my destiny lay elsewhere, I still have a warm sense of belonging whenever I go into a Press Office.

Of course, Press Offices today are very different places from those of the thirties. They are vast in size, densely populated and, above all, centres of high technology. The notebook and pencil have given way to the word processor; the fluent use of shorthand, once so essential to every aspiring young reporter, has been swept aside in favour of the tape recorder. How different it all was at the office in London Street.

The building itself was a credit to the men who built it. Mind you, anything would have been an improvement on the drab, featureless building which preceded it on the site. I have no knowledge of the architect, but it was Thomas Yelf and his men who, from their depot at Thorpe Station, carried out the transformation. First they brought great loads of wooden scaffold poles and interminable lengths of rope with which to lash them.

20

Number 57 London Street, September 5th 1899.

The Press Office under construction, November 14th 1900.

Then, out came the sash windows and the bill sticker's paradise which constituted the ground floor; in went the five graceful arches at the bottom and the little dormers at the top. Then, in the fullness of time, it was revealed as a building fit to grace what became known as Norwich's Bond Street.

When it was first opened, in 1901, it was hailed as being the last word in provincial newspaper offices. I suppose the trouble was that it never moved with the times and, even in the thirties, it was still a symbol of the Victorian era, as also were many of its occupants! But it was such a friendly place.

The first person to greet the visitor was Mr. Daly, the one-armed doorman who, in his navy blue suit with its shiny brass buttons, proudly displayed his two mementoes of the Great War — an empty sleeve and a chest bedecked with medal ribbons. Then, once inside, one came face to face with Winnie Blowers who, apart from the charlady, was the only female member of the staff. She it was who operated the rather primitive switchboard and typed such letters as it was considered necessary to type, which was not many.

The manager of the Front Office was Herbert Perry, about whom I most remember his red nose and the flower in his buttonhole — a fresh one every day and always grown by himself. His self-appointed mission in life seemed to be to save the Norfolk News Company as much expense as possible and he doled out notebooks and pencils as though the very action caused him pain. When a young reporter applied for a new pencil, he was required to present the old one for inspection — if it was still more than an inch long, he was told to go away and not be wasteful.

But it was the men who worked in the back rooms who made the place so unique. There was something distinctive about reporters in those days. They were, almost without exception, eccentric characters, although the extent of their eccentricity seems greater in retrospect than it did when they were busily scribbling their 'copy'. Perhaps, in years to come, the same will be said of today's breed of journalists.

I suppose one should start at the top with the Editor — there was no editor-in-chief in those days. When the creation of such a post had been suggested, the Chief Reporter, who habitually dropped his h's, dismissed the idea out of hand, saying "There's only one editor and thass Mr. 'Ardy". Mr. 'Ardy was, in fact, Archie Cozens-Hardy, a tall, thin man who appeared to me to be very reserved, almost shy. And he had the strange habit of always wearing mittens as he sat at his desk. I think it must have been because of bad circulation for, on the one occasion when he shook hands with me, it was rather like being grabbed by a wet codfish.

But it was the Reporters' Room which had the greatest attraction for me, for it was populated by a group of larger-than-life characters, the like of which I have never encountered anywhere else. No two men were alike, yet each could readily have stepped straight out from the pages of a Trollope novel; indeed, many could well have graced the writings of Dickens.

The room itself was almost Dickensian in style. Brown lino covered the floor, horsehair upholstery provided the only comfort and, strewn all around, there was a mass of papers of every description. It was the sort of room to which the charlady must have given no more than the traditional 'lick and a promise' — always assuming, of course, that she was allowed access to the place, which was highly unlikely.

It was not the most hospitable of rooms and I suppose it is not surprising that, as I soon discovered, the more senior occupants tended to enjoy their moments of relaxation elsewhere. On going to the office with a message for my father, I was told that he was at the branch office and had been sent for. This rather puzzled me, for I was not aware that there was such a thing as a branch office. It was only later that I discovered that the place in question was the Festival House, that ancient city hostelry so conveniently situated across the road from the back door of the office.

I believe these periodic desertions of the journalistic nest were not strictly within the company's code of practice, but the higher-ups knew all about it and were content to turn a blind eye to the practice. Joe Harrison, who later graced the eastern fringes of the circulation area at Yarmouth, recalled an occasion when, as a 16-year-old apprentice, he sat alone in the Reporters' Room practising his shorthand. Suddenly, the editor entered and demanded to know where all the reporters had gone. Joe, remaining true to his boyhood code of honour, replied, "I'm afraid, sir, they're all out on engagements".

"Is that so?" replied Mr. Cozens-Hardy. "Well, just nip across to the Festival House and find one, will you?"

The Chief Reporter was old Fred Spilling, the son of a former editor, and he sat at a high desk facing the windows, with his back to everybody else. The windows really gave little benefit as regards either light value or scenic interest, for they looked out onto the brick wall of the next-door building. On the desk before him lay "The Book", the well-thumbed diary of events which had to be covered each day by the reporters. The Book was a sacred volume around which the life of everybody in the Reporters' Room revolved. It was, indeed, the Chief Reporter's Bible.

Fred Spilling's habitual dropping of h's was a deliberate action on his part — he knew he was a character, and this was all part of the act. His deafness, however, was genuine enough, though, while exhorting his colleagues to speak up, he seemed to think it was also necessary for him to use the full power of his lungs when he wanted something done.

His use of the telephone was a joy to watch and would, I think, have made a good music hall sketch. He never quite came to terms with that new-fangled instrument and, when the bell rang, he would pick up the receiver and bellow at the mouthpiece "'Allo". There would be a slight pause while he transferred it to his better ear, and then came another full-throated "'Allo". Another pause, and then "Well, who are yer? What d'yer want?" Then, in desperation, he would shout to anybody who happened to be in the room, "Come 'ere and tell me what this stupid old fool is saying — I can't 'ear 'im".

Fred Spilling must have been well into his sixties when I first encountered him and he remained in office until he was eighty, when my father succeeded him and became guardian of The Book.

I think one could be forgiven for thinking that the needs of a local newspaper would best be served by writers with a local background, but it is not necessarily so, nor was it even in those earlier years. Indeed, one recalls a number of 'foreigners' who served the paper long and well and did much to develop it into the sort of publication it now is.

There was Handel Mills, a thin, dark Welshman who, in his dark suit and white starched collar with rounded ends, presented more than a passing likeness to a chapel preacher. He is reputed to have accused East Anglians of being dull and unimaginative, but I think he rather liked living among us — why, otherwise, would he have stayed for thirty years? Like most Welshmen, he had a tremendous love of both music and sport, but this love sometimes brought problems. I have been told by those who worked with him

Gentlemen of the Press.

Left to right: Arthur Bagshaw, John Taggart, Harry Walters (standing), Fred Spilling, Handel Mills.

that to see him trying to cope with the affairs of the day when, that very night, a symphony concert at St. Andrew's Hall clashed with some promising boxing at the Corn Hall was to observe a soul in utter torment.

Then there was John Taggart, a rather corpulent Lancastrian who came to Norwich in his youth, became a naturalised Norfolkman, yet still retained many characteristics of his home county. This applied particularly to food, and the amazing tradition which he introduced of huge tripe suppers in various city hostelries is now almost a part of local folklore. His full name was John Henry Scott-Taggart but, though his colleagues called him John, I had reason to address him by a different title, for reasons which I will explain.

One of the first assignments he was given when he joined the *E.D.P.* was to accompany another young reporter, a local man, to cover the Ideal Homes Exhibition in the Agricultural Hall. Whilst there, his eyes fell upon a pair of attractive young ladies, and he pointed them out to his colleague.

"I'll introduce you, if you like", said the Norwich man. "I know one of them".

The two girls were sisters — Emily and Mary Mace, daughters of a local businessman — and the young Norwich reporter was already 'walking out' with Emily. His name was Arthur Bagshaw and, when he was 21 and she just 19, they married; then, ten years later, they brought me into the world. Meanwhile, romance blossomed with the other pair. They married, and John Henry Taggart became simply — my Uncle Harry.

My early encounters with Uncle Harry, as a very small child, were slightly awesome affairs. He was a very big man, in head as well as body, and then there was his bulldog, which never seemed to leave his side. It was my first close encounter with a bulldog and I knew the breed had the reputation of being somewhat fearsome creatures. Then, as I studied the pair of them, I felt sure I could detect more than a passing similarity in their features. But I needn't have worried. It was that permanent twinkle in my uncle's eyes that gave the game away. Before long it became apparent that the pair of them, man and dog, were just a couple of old softies. Indeed, I developed quite a pride in my Uncle Harry, for he cut a fine figure in his brown boots and grey spats, with his silver-topped walking stick and, on Sundays, his monocle. I never could understand why he only seemed to wear a monocle on Sundays!

It was a time when almost every reporter smoked a pipe and carried a walking stick, but there were a few exceptions as regards the smoking habit. Herbert Leeds, that great columnist of the *Eastern Evening News*, was a cigarette man, while there were at least two who clung to the old habit of taking snuff. Cecil Knights, who specialised in agricultural matters and went on his rounds looking — and speaking — like a true Norfolk rustic, took it in almost heaped spoonfuls in a most explosive manner. Robert Cook, on the other hand, sniffed the most minute quantities with a degree of grace that had to be seen to be believed. I was quite a small boy when I first witnessed the delicate manner in which the operation was carried out, and I stood entranced in admiration. But, of course, Bob Cook did everything with a bit of style. His usual dress consisted of a Norfolk jacket of blue serge, with black and white check trousers and a big, floppy, black bow tie — quite unique. But it was his writing which most served to single him out from the rest. Surely he must have been one of the greatest users of the King's English ever to grace the pages of the *E.D.P.*

Away from the Reporters' Room, the two chief sub-editors of the day were Tom Burley and Fred Bill. Tom and Fred shared many nocturnal sessions cutting down the reporters' work to fit the needs of the paper, and they also found time every night to engage in interminable games of dominoes. They kept a running score right through their association and, when Tom's death brought the game to a sudden end, it was said that the points total ran into hundreds of thousands, with not more than thirty between them.

Harry Walters was Chief Photographer and a man of divine talent. Indeed, I have always looked upon him as being the first in a long line of such men whose work has illuminated the pages of the *E.D.P.* He had an artificial leg, but it never seemed to handicap him in his work. He was, in fact, so agile that I doubt whether many people ever noticed. But he was, above all, a man of great humanity and understanding, and I shall never forget the night when I was on the receiving end of one of his great acts of kindness.

It was in the fifties when, being deeply involved in amateur dramatics, I was producing a string of shows for the Wymondham Players. It was always my custom to write in advance to the Chief Photographer with the request that that one of his men attend the dress rehearsal to take a few photographs — they were valuable publicity when the review appeared in the paper. The young photographer would duly arrive; we would stop the rehearsal and take up various poses so that he could get two or three shots; then he would be off, as quickly as he had come, to some other town or village where his services were required.

On the night in question, however, things went rather differently. I was just about to leave home to go to the W. I. Hall when the telephone rang. It was Harry Walters, covered in confusion, apologising for the fact that all his photographers were out on assignments and thus unable to get to Wymondham. To save us from disappointment, however, he proposed to come over and take the photographs himself − if that was alright with me. If it was alright, indeed! By the time he arrived at the Hall we were about ten minutes into the rehearsal. I offered to halt the proceedings so that he could take his pictures and then get away, but he would have none of it.

"If it's alright with you", he said, "I'd like to stop and see the show − we can get the pictures later".

And he did just that. For the one and only time, we gave a performance to an audience of one. And what a splendid audience he was − he laughed in all the right places and applauded at the end of every scene. When the final curtain came down, he came to me with fulsome praise.

"I really enjoyed that", he said. "You've got a real success on your hands. Now, how about getting some pictures?"

He set about his task with such unhurried calm and patient attention to detail that it was past eleven o'clock when he finally left the W. I. Hall. And the pictures were great.

Those, then, were the men I met during my visits to the old Press Office. They were a small, intimate company and they were all incredibly kind. There were others I should have mentioned, not least my own father, but I prefer to leave that to others lest I be accused of bias. And there were so many who followed in the footsteps of those I have described and who became much-loved friends. Men like Cliff Butler, Stephen Amyes and Eric Fowler − three men with kind hearts and great talent.

They all had a pride in their craft which, I think, is best summed up in the words of Eric Fowler. "You can't get away with just any old rubbish in the *E.D.P.*", he said. "If you try, the readers will tell you about it before you've got halfway along London Street in the morning".

Perhaps, some day, somebody will write a history of the *Eastern Daily Press*. I hope so, for those old memories are too precious to be lost.

CHAPTER 3

Café Royal and Mugs' Hall.

The building adjoining the old Press Office in London Street, separated only by a narrow passage-way leading to a billiards hall, was the home of another concern which became very much a local institution. This was the Café Royal, that unique continental restaurant so lovingly run for two generations by the Rayna family.

It was Cristofero Fasola who, in 1887, had taken over the former insurance offices and transformed them into an eating place which, for over half a century, was to become a much-loved centre of the social life of the city. He had previously run similar establishments in Bournemouth and Brighton, but the concept of wining and dining in such continental style was something entirely new to Norwich. Italian chefs and waiters, menus set out in French, and a genial proprietor who bowed invitingly to each individual visitor were something of a novelty, and the Café Royal quickly became the favourite restaurant among professional and business people of both city and county. Then there was the fact that Cristofero was a keen yachtsman, and it was not long before the sailing fraternity were beating a path to his door. The business flourished to such a degree that, after only eight years in London Street, the popular host was able to return to his native Switzerland to enjoy the fruits of his labours in what proved to be a lengthy retirement.

His departure in 1895 signalled the arrival of a man who had earlier worked with him at Bournemouth and Brighton. He was Carlo Angelo Rayna, a man who took great pride in carrying on the business in the style of his predecessor. Carlo had been born in Milan, leaving school at the age of ten and working for a time for a constructional engineering company in Germany.

This proved not to his liking and, at the age of seventeen, his parents sent him to England to learn both the English language and the business of catering.

On arriving in London Street, Carlo, with the help of his wife, soon increased even further the popularity of the establishment. He had all the winning manners of the polished Continental, coupled with a most friendly disposition. His keen sense of humour

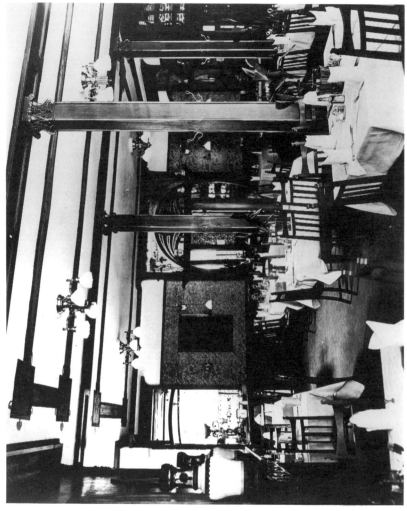

The continental splendour of the Café Royal.

also appealed to his customers, who frequently asked him to join them at their table for coffee and cigars. But, above all, he set the standards of excellence which made the Royal a mecca for the county's *bon viveurs.*

Snow-white linen adorned the tables, albeit occasionally bedecked with indelible, yet homely, purple wine stains. In the rather muted daylight, the cutlery gleamed like moonshine; then, when the artificial light was brought into use, the effect was like the sparkle of quicksilver. Amidst all this show of style, and against a background of mahogany panelling, the waiters moved around with quiet discretion, serving their favourite diners and forever remaining aware of the wishes and foibles of each and every one. My late friend, Stanley Woolf, stayed as a guest for two years at the Café Royal and described it in his own inimitable style. "It was", he said, "a gourmet's caravanserai, an exotic fragment of Soho lifted up and planted in the heart of Norwich".

Over the years, quite a number of the employees grew old and grey in the Raynas' service, and they were such delightful characters. Luigi, a swarthy, curly-headed little man with all the arts of the born waiter, was a popular and amusing figure. He balanced dishes like a conjurer and was a lightning reckoner when it came to making out a customer's bill. Then there was Cesare Carreta, volcanic and unpredictable, and always sporting that magnificently tended moustache. And there right to the end was old Romeo Paggani, bent and grumbly, forever peering over his crazy Will Hay spectacles; a bit decrepit, but capable of sudden explosions of sardonic wit.

Oddly enough, it was two of the more humble members of the staff who lingered most in my old friend Stanley's memory. "First", he said, "there was Ernest the kitchen boy, with his narrow, grinning face, who watered the flower baskets in summer and sprinkled circles of coolness on the hot pavement. Then, Wilfred the pantryman, whom I saw one morning careering down late from his attic room, his chamber pot in one hand and his false teeth in the other".

But, of course, there were many more characters among the clientele than among the staff, for they converged on the place from every quarter and from every walk of upper and middle class life. The Church was well represented, as were the County families and the learned professions. Titles, it was said, were two a penny. Farmers flocked there for lunch on Saturdays, and there was one

London Street, showing the Press Office and the Café Royal, 1932.

33

among their number who regularly attended for his afternoon refreshment of a pot of tea and a round of toast. Unfortunately, there were times when he had perhaps already partaken rather too freely of something a bit stronger, and his befuddled mind demanded "a round of tea and a pot of toast".

Many societies met there for their annual dinners, and at the time of the Norfolk and Norwich Triennial Music Festival eminent conductors and artistes were to be seen at the tables. There were many great nights at the Café Royal, but two which lived long in the memory of people who were there were the celebration parties on Mafeking Night and on Armistice Night 1918. In March 1900 there had been the occasion when a complimentary dinner was given to Mr. George Gilbert, whose circus at the Agricultural Hall drew full houses on every night of a three-month run. One of the special dishes on that occasion was 'Bombe à la Circus; anchois sur toast à la George Gilbert, extra devilled'.

Fred Morgan, the proprietor of the old Theatre Royal, was a daily caller for oysters when in season. He and his host had much in common, for Carlo was a great lover of the stage and particularly of grand opera. Finally there was that renowned figure of the Turf, Fred Dowson (of whom, more later). For years, up to within a fortnight of his death, he lunched and dined at the Café Royal. Indeed, it was long claimed in the kitchen that his life had been prolonged by the care taken to provide him with such dishes as his declining health required.

Thus the years passed and the Café Royal thrived as part of the Norwich social scene. Carlo, with his wife and family, always lunched and dined in the restaurant and he regularly kept Christmas Day there as a family gathering in which the entire staff were invited to join. In his leisure time he enjoyed his gramophone records of Italian operatic artistes and, in summer, his yachting and fishing. And then there was his motoring, for he was one of the city's first owner-drivers. Frequently, on a Sunday afternoon, he would suggest a drive out into the country, usually to Bramerton Woods End. As the magnificent De Dion carried its passengers down Prince of Wales Road, the city folk out promenading would stop, look and wave, for motor cars were not yet very numerous. Then, on the return trip, the same promenaders would give them a round of applause as if in congratulation at having successfully completed such a long and hazardous journey.

Ironically, it was the increasing use of motor cars which

threatened the continued existence of the Café Royal. By the summer of 1930, Carlo's health had begun to fail, and he handed over the reins to his son, Stanley Enrico Rayna. Stanley, educated at Norwich Grammar School and trained in the restaurant business in Naples, Rome and London, maintained the traditions of the place, but a marked change in eating habits was already perceptible. Professional and business people who formerly had either lunched or dined at the Royal tended more and more to drive home for meals, and those who continued to come demanded simpler fare.

Stanley maintained the wide range of dishes and the extensive wine list, but the people of city and county gradually failed to respond to the lure of the Café Royal. After so many years it all had to end. Stanley accepted the inevitable, but decided to bow out in style with a tremendous dinner. They came to that alright, for every table was booked long before the event.

So it was that, on Saturday, March 26th 1938, the Raynas entertained their final guests. The last dinner party was served, the final cork drawn, the ultimate reveller helped on with his overcoat. Then it was all over. My old friend was left with his memory of Stanley Rayna as a dear and good friend, a gentle and generous host with the endearing habit of playing Neapolitan airs on his fiddle which he held upside down like a cello on his knee.

Looking at what has now taken the place of the Café Royal, one is left with only the memory of all the rich conviviality that went on within those walls, and of that warm, close family who were at the heart of it all. Alas, one looks back upon a vision of Paradise lost.

But the year the old place closed was 1938 − the year of Munich. Fate was on the trail of each and every one of us. The war came and, in due course, the Americans . . . How they would have loved the Café Royal!

At this point I feel we must withdraw our attention from London Street and transfer our thoughts to Thorpe Road, for it is there, at number 22, that we can recall the memory of that wealthy bookmaker who dined at the Café Royal. His name was Dicky Dowson and he was one of the great Norwich characters of the Victorian and Edwardian eras. To say that he was larger than life would be an understatement − they really did throw away the mould after he had been made.

Of his parentage and upbringing I know little, except that when he was born, in 1859, he was given the name Fred (a name which few people used), and that his first efforts at earning a living were as a painter and decorator. It was while he was engaged in this occupation that he discovered a useful method of supplementing his income — by taking small bets from his workmates and, indeed, from anybody else who fancied a wager. This sideline rapidly became so successful that he gave up house painting and concentrated solely on being a bookie. It was obviously a wise decision for, by the time he was thirty, he had become the greatest bookmaker in the Eastern Counties and a familiar figure on every racecourse in the country. With success came riches and, in 1894, he decided to build himself a Town House in keeping with his position in society. Because of his frequent countrywide travelling it is not surprising that he should choose the Thorpe Road site, directly facing the railway station on the opposite side of the road.

No expense was to be spared in the building of his new home, and he began by acquiring the services of A. F. Scott, one of the most eminent architects of Victorian Norwich. One cannot help thinking that the two men were a most unlikely pair for, while Scott was nonconformist, vegetarian and a total abstainer as regards both alcohol and tobacco, Dowson was too busy wining, dining and smoking fat cigars to pursue any deep religious belief. But both men had one great ambition — to produce a building of distinction which would be nothing less than a jewel in the city's crown. And that is just what they did, for the house they built must surely be almost unique in the domestic architecture of Norwich as an example of Victorian craftsmanship and extravagance.

Number 22 still stands, gazing out across the road towards Thorpe Station, though it is more than half a century since Dicky Dowson was carried to his final resting place and the house became the home of various business concerns. But it has been lovingly cared for, and those dramatic dark red bricks — Costessey bricks they were, much admired in their day for both durability and artistic effect — still cause it to stand out from the more restrained buildings which adjoin it. Then there are the ornamental gables and mouldings, the highly decorated terra cotta front and, in contrast, the simple flight of stone steps leading up from the street to the front door. Inside the house there are the ornately carved staircase and timbers, and the elegantly moulded ceilings under which he entertained his guests in such lavish style — not to mention the marble bath. At the back of his house he had

Kingswood House, nicknamed Mugs' Hall by its owner.

his stables and coach house, for his affection for horses was by no means based solely on the income they brought in from his clients.

When the house was completed, it was given the suitably grandiose name of Kingswood House. It was Dicky Dowson himself who, acknowledging the source of the wealth which had made it all possible, jokingly nicknamed it Mugs' Hall.

It must be said, however, that the lavishness of Mugs' Hall was not just a tawdry example of a rich man showing off his wealth. It was simply a reflection of his lifestyle, for he mixed freely with the 'upper crust', never presenting the conventional image of a bookmaker, but looking for all the world like one of the Edwardian toffs who placed their bets with him. He rode to hounds, entertained on a grand scale and, at the end of the flat-racing season, took himself off to Monte Carlo, to Paris or to Venice. But he was generous in the extreme in his support of local charities − and always anonymously.

At Newmarket he was afforded special facilities in the members' enclosure, and there was one great occasion, at a point-to-point meeting of the West Norfolk Hunt, when King Edward VII sent his equerry to him to place some bets. For a long while after that event Dicky proudly boasted that he was under royal patronage.

It was on the hunting field that Dicky Dowson first met Sir Alfred Munnings who, at that time, had set up a studio, with ample accommodation for horses, at Swainsthorpe. The encounter gave mutual pleasure to both men, but it proved to be particularly significant for Munnings, as he later acknowledged in his autobiography. He was finding great difficulty in meeting the financial demands being made upon him by such people as his tailor and his bank manager − not to mention the cost of his horses − and buyers for his paintings were not too easy to find. But Dowson's interest was stirred and the following Sunday, with his wife at his side, he drove over to Swainsthorpe in a very smart turnout with a splendid mare between the shafts. Munnings displayed his paintings and a full inspection was carried out, but no decision was made. Instead, Dowson invited him to a coursing club dinner, at which he would make known his choice. The dinner duly took place and, as the two men basked in a post-prandial glow brought on by a succulent meal and a splendid selection of good wines, Dowson named his chosen painting and handed his guest £150 in notes. At that moment, Munnings must have experienced conflicting emotions for, as he was later to write: "I had asked him £300. But the dinner, the champagne and the rustling of all the notes were too much for me, and I took the notes". The painting which Dowson had chosen was 'The Horse Fair', that delightful masterpiece which he was later to bequeath to Norwich Castle Museum.

If it is true that Dowson knew a good painting when he saw one, it was even more so with horses, and the story of the man would never be complete without mention of the mare which took him and his wife on that visit to Swainsthorpe. Her name was Glencoe Belle and, at one time, she became just as well-known in the sporting world as was her owner. She was one of a trio of Canadian trotters which had been imported by a local doctor who later regretted the expense of his action and decided to sell one. Dowson offered to buy and, having made his choice, paid the doctor £95 for Belle. As always, he made the right choice, for she proved to be tremendously fast and soon paid a handsome dividend on top of her purchase price. He won many a wager with her, the most celebrated being the occasion when, in 1899, he struck a bet of £500 with a London sportsman that she could trot ten miles in half an hour on a level stretch of turnpike road. The site chosen for the trial was a quiet, tree-shaded stretch of what is now the A11 trunk road from Larling to Attleborough and back, and the entire proceedings were supervised by a referee appointed by *Sporting Life*. It was a hot, dry evening in June and many hundreds of people turned out from Norwich and elsewhere to watch as, with clouds of dust flying all along the route, Glencoe Belle duly trotted her ten miles in a recorded time of 29 minutes 35 $^2/_5$ seconds.

It really was the end of an era when, in 1936, Dicky Dowson breathed his last. No more would he set out in the morning to tempt the punters at some distant racecourse; no more, in the evening, would he sally forth in pursuit of good food, fine wine and pleasant company. His life had spanned some 77 years, each one filled with as much true living as many men would encounter in an entire lifetime.

Dicky Dowson has gone, but he left the city of Norwich a splendid bit of heritage, for Mugs' Hall is still there — even though the present occupiers have preferred to rename it Bewick House.

CHAPTER 4

Norwich Hill.

I still cling to the belief that something of the heart went out of Norwich when they took away the old Cattle Market and transplanted it at Harford Bridges. Mind you, part of the City's agricultural soul had already gone, for the Corn Exchange had long been demolished and the Agricultural Hall was no longer fulfilling its original function. But when the City finally gave up playing host to the weekly invasion from the countryside there was little left to remind Norwich of the debt it owed to its agricultural surroundings.

For as long as any of us could remember, Saturday had been the day when Norwich became a farmyard, with all the sights and sounds — not to mention the smells — of the countryside. The cobbles of the city streets echoed to the assorted sounds of sliding hooves, hobnailed boots and clattering sticks whilst, at frequent intervals, a half-crazed beast, having escaped from its minders, would put in an appearance in some unexpected and unwelcome place.

But it was 'The Hill' which was the Saturday Mecca for the farming fraternity, just as it was for the many who went simply as onlookers or, like many a local urchin, to earn a few pence 'bullock-whopping'. And it was 'The Hill' which captivated me when, as a little boy, I viewed the scene for the very first time. At the bottom, between the Shirehall and the Agricultural Hall, there were sheep by the hundred; then came the fat cattle waiting for some local butcher to give them his stamp of approval; and, finally, the store cattle, many of them shipped over from Ireland to enjoy a slightly longer life expectancy on lush Norfolk pastures.

The entire area up to Rose Avenue was Edmund Ireland's domain. There that modest, much respected man sold fat shorthorn beasts, seemingly hour after hour, in a quiet monotone and without the slightest suggestion of histrionics. His forefinger would indicate the buyer and there was no need to call a name or even to tell his chief clerk at his elbow.

On the left, all the way up the steep slope of Cattle Market Street,

Sheep by the hundred at the bottom of the Hill.

Cattle waiting for buyers at the top.

came the snorting and grunting of a multitude of pigs of every size, gradually merging with a variety of sounds from the smaller stock — the goats and rabbits, the ferrets and the cage birds. Only then did one come to an area of comparative peace, for this was the place to buy an old barrow, a second-hand bicycle or one of the many other objects which, to my childish mind, had such a strange title — they were the 'dead stock'. Then, along the short length of Bell Avenue, there was a tightly-packed myriad of stalls, offering everything from strong, hard-wearing farm clothing to patent medicines for both man and beast. And then, of course, there was the mayhem of Spelman's Horse Sale, immortalised in the paintings of Sir Alfred Munnings.

To a little boy such as I then was, it was the most wonderful of all spectacles. It was frightening, yet alluring; smelly, yet romantic. It was inconceivable then that the tradition of the Saturday Market on Norwich Hill could ever become nothing more than just a memory. But the Market has gone, and all that remains is the memory.

To begin with, there were the demands of the motor car, spreading through the countryside like a cancerous growth, but that was only part of the story. A short while before the move was made to Harford, I went to The Hill to take a last nostalgic look at the scene which had thrilled me in my early years. I saw the same sights which that little boy had seen all those years earlier. The scene was the same, but now I was seeing it through the eyes of an adult, and a mere twenty minutes was enough to convince me that the sooner the move was made the better. Indeed, if I had been true to my conscience, I would have turned vegetarian on the spot.

In spite of my misgivings on that last visit, however, I still have the feeling that, when the Cattle Market moved to Harford, it took part of the City with it. Since then, an entire generation has known Market Hill merely as a temporary resting place for visiting motor cars. Now, an even newer generation awaits the beginning of yet another chapter with the arrival of the Castle Mall development. Thus, the days of the Cattle Market slip even further back into history, and it is only the older ones among us who still retain the memory of those long-ago Saturdays when the country came to Town. This is particularly true of the days before the motor car became the main mode of transport and when a succession of horse-drawn vehicles would converge on Norwich from all points of the compass, bringing the county folk in for a Saturday on The Hill.

One man with vivid memories of those days is Ben Burgess. Ben's father farmed at Howe and, apart from the heavy horses which worked the fields, he kept three lighter specimens for domestic duties. First place in the family's affection went to 'The Old Pony' — he had no other name, but aptly lived up to what he was called for, towards his end in the late 1920s, he was confidently believed to be 40 years old. His main duty was to power the governess cart, a square-built tub of a vehicle in which the passengers sat facing one another and sideways to the direction of travel. This transport combination was reserved for Mother and the children, or the governess, or any visiting female, and it never went any further than Trowse railway station.

Ben's father also kept two working Irish mares, one for riding and one for pulling the trap. This stoutly-built vehicle was used for longer journeys and also for the occasional transport of the smaller farm livestock. It was attractively lined out in contrasting colours of dark green and biscuit and was always kept in good condition, being regularly washed and polished at least once a week. It was this vehicle which took the family on their Saturday trips to Norwich Market.

The journey to Norwich was a very formal occasion. The start was promptly at 8-30 and it was a point of honour and good sense not to keep a horse waiting once the trap was at the front gate. Of course, Ben's father and mother sat in front and, through winter and summer alike, shared the rug. For some unknown reason it was traditional for the driver, on the off side, to have a box under his cushioned seat, thus raising him some three or four inches above his passenger. It seemed to serve no practical purpose, but may have provided status. The whip was in its holder on the right and there was also a socket for the 'gig umbrella' in the centre. The children sat facing backwards on a most uncomfortable, lightly padded, moveable board, politely called the 'dickey seat'. They had to lean forward in a crouching position and were only prevented from falling off the back by the tail board, which was actually the back of the cart let down on leather-covered chains and provided with a mat for their feet to rest against. The unfortunate youngsters were unable to share any interest in what was happening in front, and when it rained they got all the drips from the gig umbrella. For passengers on the dickey seat there was little pleasure or romance in that form of transport but, once they arrived at Pollock's Stables in Orford Place, the sights and smells of the big city amply compensated for the discomfort of the journey.

Father always sat very upright, rarely took his whip and never 'pushed' his horse. He always trotted uphill and walked downhill — and galloped never. In spite of their backward view, the journey to Norwich was full of interest for the children. They knew every tree, bush and gate, and they knew all the other travellers. Would they catch up that one? Would the other one catch them? But nothing would make father change speed. He started to walk the horse downhill at exactly the same spot and he broke into a trot again just before he came to level road. By checking the time, the boys were encouraged to calculate their average speed — rarely more than eight miles per hour.

From the top of Trowse bridge, on a dull winter's day, the family could see the smog which they would run into opposite Martineau Lane. Looking back over the years, it is difficult to appreciate the extent to which the atmosphere was polluted when the chimneys of the tightly-packed houses in the area around King Street and Ber Street were belching forth coal smoke — particularly when there was no wind to take it away.

Then, after the long haul up Bracondale, there was a choice of two routes. Ber Street was the shorter, but nice people did not use Ber Street on Saturdays; indeed, really nice people never used Ber Street at all, for it was not considered respectable. The only time Ben's father went that way was when he was in the mind to buy Irish cattle. Then he would want to see how many cattle the Irish dealers had in reserve betweeen Trowse and The Hill, in order to judge whether to buy early or late. On those occasions they were obliged to weave their way down Ber Street between bunches of cattle standing stationary on either side of the street, interspersed with small, shouting boys and large, barking dogs. Then came the tricky negotiation of Westlegate, which at that time was a narrow, dangerous little street. Normally, from Bracondale they would go a little further along over St. Catherine's Plain and down Surrey Street, which was a very respectable area. The right hand turn on entering St. Stephen's was a bit tricky but very exciting for the children, especially if there were a couple of trams blocking the roadway before they got to the stables.

Once there, the mare would swing in under the arched doorway in anticipation of the handful of oats which she knew was waiting in her regular stall at the top of the padded ramp which led to the

Spelman's Horse Sale, 1912.

first floor stabling. In retrospect, the stableyard now seems too small to accommodate all the farmers' carts which used Pollock's Stables on a Saturday, but it was all done to a system. The wheels of each new arrival went over the shafts of the previous one, and they packed in very tightly. Even so, the ostler had to know the habits of his customers — the early goers-home and the late leavers. They were all creatures of habit.

Then it was off to The Hill, making sure not to stray too far from Father's side in the hustle and bustle which was everywhere. This was a wise expedient, particularly when they reached the area near the Bell Hotel where Spelman's Horse Sale offered excitement which was hair-raising in the extreme. Indeed, Ben has never ceased to wonder why someone amongst the vast crowd of onlookers was not killed there every week of the year. Without warning, and for no apparent reason at all, a haltered horse, led by an ostler or groom resplendent in cord breeches and short waistcoat but no jacket, would charge into the crowd, the man flourishing his whip and shouting at the top of his voice. The crowd would scatter to left and right, and at the end of their run the pair would return at even greater speed, to come to an abrupt halt in front of the auctioneer. Then the bidding would start and, hopefully, would rapidly pass the reserve price. If not, the auctioneer would call for 'another show' and the whole dangerous process would be repeated. There can be little wonder why Alfred Munnings found inspiration in such a scene.

From the elevated pathway round the Castle Gardens one could look down on the whole milling mob of buyers, sellers and spectators attending Spelman's Sale. There was one man, however, who, though he stood regularly on that passageway, saw nothing of what was going on before him, for he was Blind Billy. Billy was one of the characters of old Norwich, standing for long hours with his back to the railings and with dozens of leather bootlaces hanging round his neck. The laces were black on one side and brown on the other and were still attached at the top to the cowhide from which they had been cut. It became a ritual every week to stop and have a word with Billy and to buy a pair of his laces. Ben recalls that, long after Billy was no more and even when he, himself, had given up wearing heavy laced-up boots, he still kept finding pairs of Billy's laces in odd places about the house.

From Billy's vantage point at the edge of the Castle Gardens it was just a short stroll to Ladell's Restaurant on the Walk, where the family would have lunch, consisting of a hot minced beef pie as big as the plate on which it sat, washed down with a cup of coffee. And so to the Corn Hall in Exchange Street.

No Saturday Market Day was complete without a visit to Oram and Tyce, the ironmongers in Davey Place. As far as the children were concerned, it was a real Aladdin's Cave of goodies and, while Father was buying nuts, bolts and nails, their eyes wandered longingly over sticks of solder and sheets of zinc. Then there was Watson, the chemist, to be visited, for it was from him that Father bought the raw materials to make up his own horse balls and cattle drinks. Laudanum, iodine and permanganate of potash were also part of his purchase, as were Stockholm Tar and copper sulphate for sheep foot rot. Then there were such things as baskets and skeps to be bought from William Cox, whose grandson, many years later, was still continuing the trade.

There were occasions when, somewhat reluctantly, Ben and his brothers were handed over to Mother for the afternoon, usually when they were in need of new clothing. For footwear, Rutlands of Davey Place was their supplier and, after three smalls boys had been fitted up, Mother would enquire innocently, "And how much for this quarter dozen?"

Hay Hill as George Green saw it from his outfitter's shop

But for items of general clothing there was one store which stood out from the rest — Green's, that wonderful men's outfitters which stretched through from the Walk to the Orford Hill end of White Lion Street. There seemed to be acres of space within the shop, with tailors' dummies on stands and a showcase full of stuffed King Charles Spaniels. But the showpiece of all was George Green himself, all six feet of him, with his pointed white beard and immaculate frock coat. He stood quite upright, like a drill sergeant. He had a word for every customer who came near, welcomed their enquiries and directed them to the attention of equally well-dressed shop walkers who seemed to abound. Rumour had it that he had once been Lord Mayor of Norwich — he certainly looked the part. It was an honour to wear a pair of short trousers which came from Mr. Green's shop, and every transaction was carried out with a bit of style. To think that a modern supermarket now occupies such a hallowed site!

"Never", says Ben, "have I seen such a bow as George Green was wont to give my mother with three small boys at foot. But this was the same man who could suddenly relax, shake my father's hand, call him by his Christian name and talk of old times — behind a pillar or showcase, of course. I never knew what they had in common."

Green's was one of the great Norwich institutions, as was another establishment which demanded the family's attention. This was Jarrold's Library, where the weekly visits were eagerly anticipated on two counts. First, there was the ride up in the lift, with the lift boy, his cap at a rakish angle, seemingly knowing all his customers and delivering them to the floor they needed without instructions. Then there was the sight of Miss Needham.

Miss Needham was A Character. She ruled her girl assistants like an Amazon Company Sergeant-Major. Her tight-waisted black dress swept the floor and her black net choker — supported, presumably, by whalebone — held her head in a rigid frontal-look position which necessitated an excessive amount of quick turning and twisting of the shoulders. But she was a kindly person who had a smile for small children when they were a few yards away. She could not see them easily if they were too close; her choker was so high that to look at anything close she had to bend at the waist.

Miss Needham's regular customers did not need to go searching through the ample shelves. Mother checked in the previous week's books with the assistant at the desk; Miss Needham, with a smile, then indicated the family's reading for the next week. She seemed to know all their different tastes in literature, and she never got it wrong. "Jarrold's Library", says Ben, "was never the same after Miss Needham died — died she must have done; I can't imagine Miss Needham in retirement. Of course, there's no place in modern shopkeeping for a Miss Needham or for the activities over which she reigned. Such people and activities don't provide sufficient turnover per square foot of floor space. I'm lucky to remember other days".

One of the compensations of being in the charge of Mother was that they usually arrived back at Pollock's Stables with time to spare. This meant that Ben and his brothers had the chance of sharing the roaring fire which Dick, the head ostler, stoked up in the tack room, or of creeping up the ramp to take a look at the double row of carriage horses on the first floor. Better still was the Punch and Judy Show on Orford Hill. This was a continuous performance of about half an hour, though the collection tin came round about every five minutes. Having made the mistake of dropping their pennies into the tin when it first came round, they did not like to be seen to refuse the second time, so ten minutes was about the length of their watching.

However, there was another entertainment which appeared to be free. It came in the form of a very large man with an imposing white beard and a placard which read: "Prepare To Meet Thy God". The voice of this hot gospeller could be heard as far away as the Walk. The boys had no idea what he was shouting about, but it was clear to them that they would be in for a very rough time if they didn't behave themselves.

The journey home from Pollock's Stables began with the mild excitement of turning out into the traffic in Red Lion Street. Horses which had been in a stable all day were, not unnaturally, anxious to get going on the journey home. Once loaded up and the reins in Father's hands, the ostler would lead the horse down the wooden blocks of the passage from the stableyard on to the granite setts of Red Lion Street and point the party homewards towards St. Stephen's and Surrey Street before jumping clear on to the left hand pavement. Many horses at that point used to show their pleasure by taking the first few steps with forefeet in the air. Nothing was done to discourage this manoeuvre — it cleared the populace out of the way and showed that they had a horse with spirit. Care had to be taken at the sharp left turn into Surrey Street. It was as well to be sure that one's wheels were not in the St. Stephen's tramlines when the turn was started, and the boys at the back were warned to hang on tight to the side chains to avoid being thrown out.

And so, in winter, began the cold journey home. The rug around the passengers' knees required constant attention and, if it was raining, evasive action was needed to avoid the drips from the large gig umbrella. Strangely enough, Ben can never remember the journey in summertime — it always seemed to be dark as they drove across Howe Common. Then, from his cottage, Albert Symonds would hear their approach and beat them to the front door to catch the reins with one hand as he took the bridle with the other. There was no need to open the front door either — the rest of the family were there, out of curiosity tinged with excitement, to help unload the parcels and carry them into the house.

And so to high tea and — as another man was known to say — so to bed.

CHAPTER 5

Hidden Places.

The L.O.C.

I suppose the idea of a men-only coffee shop would be regarded as something of an anachronism in present-day society, but the Victorians saw things rather differently. The men of that era preferred to engage in their discussions away from the distractions of female company, and the womenfolk, passively accepting the situation, were left to do their gossiping elsewhere. So, right through the Edwardian age and beyond, those bastions of male isolationism flourished, with the waitresses being the only females permitted within their walls.

Then came a gradual change in social life, particularly in the years between the wars, and steadily, one by one, the coffee shops became open house to one and all. But there was one such establishment which, by convention rather than edict, strove to maintain its all-male tradition right through until 1960, and that was the L.O.C. It was always known by that title, and it was some years before I realised that the initials stood for Lambert's Oriental Café.

In the early years of the century when those renowned blenders of coffee, tea and tobacco had started setting up their chain of shops in the city, one of their prime sites was in the then-blossoming London Street. On one side of it stood Langfords, where Louis Marchesi was offering cakes and confectionery as good as any in Norwich; on the other, adjoining Opie Street, was the salon of R. V. Bennekom, the ladies' hairdresser. The shop front which greeted passers-by was a wonderful example of Victorian fussiness — one cannot help wondering what happened to it when the place was modernised in more recent times. The interior of the shop, packed with the end-products of a variety of oriental leaves and beans, was heavy with a pot-pourri of eastern aromas which wafted out on to London Street. But it was down in the basement where the city's business and professional men met for their morning coffee, a ritual presided over by Miss Tuck and her assistant, known only as Edna.

Lambert's Oriental Café.

Going to the L.O.C. was rather like joining a club, except that the mere fact of joining carried no privileges. One had to be a fairly regular attender over a period of a month or two before one was accepted by the established habitués of the place, and that is why I never really became a member. It was in the fifties, at a time when my contact with Norwich was limited to only one morning per week, that I paid just two visits and, to be perfectly honest, neither of them was accomplished without a certain degree of embarrassment.

My first visit was prompted by a feeling of curiosity arising from a conversation with Eric Fowler, that delightful writer whose Jonathan Mardle essays gave such pleasure to readers of the *Eastern Daily Press*. Eric was a member, and his description of the strange coffee shop and the bizarre characters who frequented it gave me the urge to see it for myself. It was when I was halfway down the stairs on that first visit that panic struck, for there in that haven of Victoriana were two groups of men sitting on old wooden settles and engaged in earnest conversation. The only vacant seat was by the side of a small table tucked away in a corner, far removed from the regulars, and I was faced with the need for a quick decision — was it to be that seat or a hasty retreat? It was then that I heard the sound of a familiar voice. It was dear Eric, inviting me to squeeze on to the settle beside him and calling to Edna to bring another cup of coffee. His announcement of my identity to his colleagues was greeted with what I considered to be a marked lack of enthusiasm, and I cannot, in all honesty, say that I felt relaxed in the situation in which I found myself. But at least I was witnessing one of the sights of old Norwich.

There was never any deliberate attempt at preventing women from visiting the L.O.C.; no notices saying "Men Only" or anything of that nature. It was simply a tradition, well-known to local people over the years. When any members of the fair sex mistakenly found their way down those stairs, there was something — some sort of aura — which quickly communicated to them a strange feeling of guilt. It so happened that two such ladies, obviously holidaymakers, arrived during my first visit. Eric tapped me on the arm.

"Watch this", he said. "They won't last long".

And he was right. The aura had got to them and, after gulping down their coffee in unseemly haste, they almost fell over each other in their dash up the stairs to freedom.

I felt a certain bond of sympathy with those two ladies when I paid my second visit to the L.O.C., for Eric Fowler was not there, and there was no welcoming invitation to join the members on one of the settles. Edna remembered me, but I took my coffee at the little table in the corner and, with an assumed air of nonchalance, climbed the stairs back into the welcoming arms of London Street.

It was only a few years later that the regulars received the sad news that the L.O.C. was to be modernised in an effort to attract a wider clientele. The old place had remained almost unchanged for half a century, mainly because they liked it as it was. Even when the big fireplace had been bricked up and replaced with a gas fire there had been signs of mutiny until they grudgingly admitted that it did provide more even heat. When Edna had been supplied with a modern percolator, they took quite a bit of convincing that the coffee really did taste as nice as when Miss Tuck had made it in her antique Victorian urn. But they stood by the place to the bitter end. Indeed, it is recorded that, even on the day when holes were drilled in the wall and the massive mantelpiece was brought crashing to the ground, one of the more senior members sat unmoved in his corner seat, drinking his coffee and reading the *Financial Times* as the air around him hung heavy with powdered plaster and brick dust.

The Nest.

Norwich City Football Club came into existence in 1902 but, after only a few years at their Newmarket Road Ground, they began to look around for somewhere more in keeping with their burgeoning status as members of the Southern League. The reason why they settled on Rosary Road for their new home has always seemed to me to be one of life's unsolved mysteries. For a sport which demands a reasonably level playing area, that elevated spot between Chalk Hill and the grandly-named Thorpe Heights must have been just about the most hostile setting they could have chosen. But chose it they did, and they set to work to excavate vast quantities of earth to produce a pitch which would meet the demands of the League. This was to become The Nest, that quaint, homely spot where the Canaries were destined to do battle for the next 27 years.

Admittedly, the fact that the site was a disused chalk pit meant that much of the excavation had already been done, but a fifty-foot concrete wall was needed at the far end to prevent the bank from

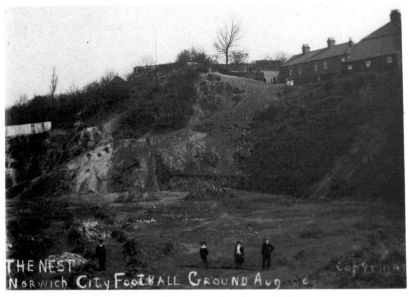

The Nest under construction, August 1908.

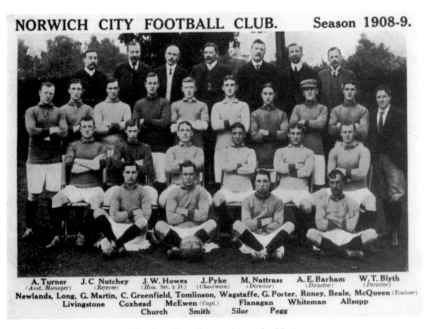

NORWICH CITY FOOTBALL CLUB.   Season 1908-9.

A. Turner   J. C. Nutchey   J. W. Howes   J. Pyke   M. Nattrass   A. E. Barham   W. T. Blyth
(Asst. Manager)   (Referee)   (Hon. Sec. & D.)   (Chairman)   (Director)   (Director)   (Director)
Newlands, Long, G. Martin, C. Greenfield, Tomlinson, Wagstaffe, G. Porter, Roney, Beale, McQueen (Trainer)
Livingstone   Coxhead   McEwen (Capt.)   Flanagan   Whiteman   Allsopp
Church   Smith   Silor   Pegg

The first Canaries to play at the Nest.

collapsing. Then, at the Rosary Road end, the added earth raised the ground to half the height of the group of nearby houses. It was one of these houses which was brought into use to serve as offices and dressing rooms. The teams changed into their playing gear in what had previously been the bedroom and, with a balcony having been added, made their entry out of the window and down a short ladder to the pitch.

When they moved from Newmarket Road, the Canaries took just two things with them. One was the grandstand, a rather modest affair little better than a garden shed, which they installed on the side of the new ground adjoining Thompson's Chalk Hill Works. The other was the Canaries' anthem, an equally modest composition, yet one which was known to rouse the players to unbelievable extremes of endeavour until the arrival of "On The Ball, City". The following four lines give some idea of the offering which had inspired the team during the six years of their stay at Newmarket Road:

> "To our Norwich City we mean to bring fame;
> With our Norwich City we'll play such a game
> That Fulham and Tottenham will faint at the name
> Of the Norwich Canaries, what-ho!"

It looks rather uninspiring in print, but I feel sure the effect was just the reverse when it issued from the throats of the supporters who packed the area behind the goal on Spion Kop. Almost every football ground had its Spion Kop, taking its name from the rocky, flat-topped hill in South Africa where so many men had been killed in battle prior to the Relief of Ladysmith a few years earlier. Norwich's Kop was the steeply terraced area between the pitch and the concrete wall at the back of the ground. A smaller wall, some eight feet in height, separated it from the playing area, and this obstacle, being so close to the pitch, was always reckoned to be worth a goal start to the Canaries. They knew how closely they could approach it without fear of collision; visiting players, however, either kept well clear of it or, in their enthusiasm, knocked themselves unconscious against it.

On the side of the ground opposite the stand was the Chicken Run, an enclosure with wooden palings along the front, corrugated iron at the sides and wire netting fixed to tall scaffold poles at the back. The purpose of the wire netting was not to control the crowd but to stop the ball from being kicked out of the ground. The adjoining property was a wood yard and, as it was always closed on Saturday afternoons, any ball which landed there could not be retrieved until the following Monday morning.

It goes without saying that the business of running a team like Norwich City in those early years was a far cry from today's high-powered operation. I recall a conversation, many years ago, with a Canary of the twenties, during which he told me that the Club paid him £3 per week during the playing season, with a reduction to £2 as a kind of retaining fee during the summer. But, in spite of such low expenses, the Canaries were always struggling to make ends meet for, even when they were admitted to the Third Division (South), they were rubbing shoulders with such lowly sides as Aberdare Athletic, Merthyr Town and Gillingham — hardly names to conjure with in the footballing world. Indeed, things became so bad in 1924 that the directors launched a public appeal for cash to keep the club solvent. A 'shilling fund' was established and the loyal fans dipped into their pockets to enable the Club to reach its target of 50,000 coins — £2,500. One wonders how far such largesse would go in the affairs of present-day football.

But some of today's expenses did not exist in the twenties. I cannot remember, for instance, any occasion when there was a marked 'police presence' at a match. There may have been the odd constable lurking somewhere, but nothing more. Then there was the question of stewarding, and this was more or less in the hands of one man. No matter how large the crowd, he packed them in single-handed. That man was Freddy Smith, a Yorkshireman who was employed by the Education Committee as drawing master for all the city's schools. He went from one school to another, spending half a day at each in turn, and thus he became well-known to all the youngsters of the city. He was also very popular, and he packed in the crowds by simply walking round the ground and pointing his pencil to indicate the action he wanted. And it never failed.

There was, of course, no such thing as a physiotherapist or a club doctor, but the Club did its best to keep the players fit and able to give of their best. This was particularly evident before an important match when, on the Friday afternoon, a wagonette would be hired to take the players for a ride out into the country around Plumstead to get some fresh air into their lungs. Anybody who remembers the smoke-laden air of the city in those early days will realise that this was not as stupid as it now sounds.

The first match at the Nest, September 1st 1908.

The last match — against Arsenal, May 6th 1935.

The Canaries got off to a good start in their first match at the Nest, beating Fulham 2—1 in a friendly encounter on September 1st 1908. At the end of the season, however, they found themselves languishing third from bottom of the league, having suffered on the way a humiliating 10—2 defeat at Swindon, which surely must still constitute something of a club record. But, on the credit side, they had caused a bit of a sensation by defeating First Division Liverpool 1—0 in the F.A. Cup.

That first friendly match had attracted a crowd of 3,300. For the final match at the Nest, on May 6th 1935, 15,550 people packed themselves in like sardines for a visit from the mighty Arsenal. The Canaries suffered a 1—0 defeat, but the result was largely irrelevant, for it was a Hospital Cup match and over £800 was raised for charity. It was, furthermore, a day of all-round celebration for, at the end of the game, both teams remained on the pitch to join with the crowd in listening to the King's Jubilee broadcast on the wireless.

So an era reached its close and, after 27 years, the Canaries left their tight little nest and sought pastures new at Carrow Road. They left behind just memories, now buried beneath an industrial estate — memories of men like Jack Vinall, Stan Ramsey, Harry Duke and, perhaps the greatest of them all, Sheringham's own Joe Hannah.

The Rosary.

Not many yards from the former hurly burly of the Nest lies another of the hidden places of Norwich and one which, with its haunting beauty and sheer tranquillity, could not possibly offer a greater contrast. It is the Rosary Cemetery where, on a well-wooded hillside, so many of our Victorian ancestors came to their final resting place. In my view, the Rosary is one of the treasures of Norwich, yet visitors never see it and few of the city's residents go there nowadays — indeed, many of them are probably unaware of its existence. Yet there, on that Thorpe Hamlet hill, lie those five acres in which is encapsulated so much of the city's earlier history. And it is more than just a burial ground — it is a sleeping beauty of a garden, though not in the way of modern cemeteries. There are neither closely-cropped lawns nor regimented rows of rose bushes, for this is nature's garden. Above the winding pathways, the forest trees — the beeches, the oaks and the chestnuts — spread themselves in a protective canopy whilst,

The woodland beauty of the Rosary.

down below, the flowers are foxgloves and campions, ox-eye daisies and the wonderfully fragrant winter heliotrope which, tradition tells us, was planted on the first day and has thrived there ever since.

Perhaps I should admit to a degree of personal bias, for my own parents lie there, as also do several generations of my ancestors. But there, also, are the mortal remains of so many of the men and women who, in life, made Norwich the city it is today. There are mayors and sheriffs, physicians and men of letters, captains of industry and illustrious members of the art world. There are the Gurneys and the Tilletts, the Colmans and the Mottrams. John Jarrold was buried there in 1852, twenty years after bringing his printing business from Woodbridge to Norwich. James Stark, of the Norwich School, lies in the Rosary under the kind of trees which he lovingly portrayed on his canvasses. And there is Emanuel Cooper, who had a massive stone sepulchre built at the top of the hill some years before his death and who derived great pleasure from going there on Sunday afternoons and sitting in it,

Ostentation – Memorial to John Barker, Steam Circus Proprietor, accidentally killed on Norwich Cattle Market, April 12th 1897.

Simplicity — R. H. Mottram's memorial by the side of the family plot.

smoking his pipe and contemplating his end. Then, of course, there is the tomb of the man who made it all possible, a retired Presbyterian minister named Thomas Drummond.

It was 1819 and, up to that time, it was the custom for all deceased persons, whatever their religious beliefs, to be buried in the churchyards of the parishes in which they lived. This meant that, with the steadily increasing population, the mediaeval churchyards were becoming grossly over-populated and they steadily rose higher and higher above the surrounding streets. It also meant that dissenters had no alternative to being buried in accordance with the rites of a church to which, in life, they had not conformed. The Reverend Mr. Drummond was one such man, and he decided that something must be done about it. Accordingly, he parted with most of his life's savings to buy five acres of what was then a market garden and to transform it into a burial ground "based upon the broad principle of Christian equality". He, himself, was not destined to be buried there for another thirty years, for he lived to the highly respectable age of 88 and was thus able to witness the early popularity of his woodland garden where all men, in death, were equal.

In accordance with his wishes, the Rosary was administered by a board of trustees, a situation which only ceased when it was entrusted to Norwich Corporation in 1956. Even then, its link with Thomas Drummond was not forgotten, for part of the agreement was that a wreath should be placed on the founder's tomb every year on the anniversary of his death. It somehow seems fitting that the last chairman of the trustees should have been R. H. Mottram, that illustrious writer and historian, who was eventually laid to rest in the family plot at the Rosary in 1971. There, having attained the age of 87, he joined the men and women whose lives he had studied and about whom he had written with such authority.

Now, on the flat top of the hill, a new cemetery steadily fills with row upon row of graves laid out in perfect symmetry in modern fashion. But the old Rosary remains what it always was — a wild, wooded garden, gently kept in check by the men who tend it. There is no symmetry. Up above, the woodland trees reach ever further upwards to the sky; below, in the shade of their branches, the country flowers come and go with the seasons. A robin trills his silvery song from the top of a monument, while squirrels dart between the tombstones, seeking hiding places for their harvest of acorns.

The Rosary is a little bit of Victorian England, hidden away from the frenetic haste of modern times. What more could any man wish than that his mortal remains should rest until eternity in such a spot?

CHAPTER 6

Forgotten Heroes.

There can be little doubt that life in Norwich in 1915 was a solemn affair. The war in Europe, which everybody had said would be over by the previous Christmas, dragged on, bringing with it more carnage amongst the fighting men and increasing tension and distress for those left at home. The young men enlisted, the young fathers, then the middle-aged; and sorrowfully, yet with a haunted pride, the people saw one name follow another in the lists of the fallen marked upon the rolls of honour in the churches.

The people of Norwich, in common with those throughout the land, searched desperately for anything to keep up their spirits. Public entertainment, much of it with a decidedly patriotic bias, continued, but what the public needed most of all was good news from the Western Front. But there was little enough of that, and they could do no more than console themselves with the continuous statements from people in authority that all would be well.

Then, on June 10th, all this was to change and, for two brief days, their spirits were to be lifted and their cares forgotten as they welcomed a local hero back in their midst for a short visit. He was Company Sergeant-Major Harry Daniels, the first Norwich man to receive the nation's supreme award for gallantry, the Victoria Cross. To be strictly accurate, Harry Daniels was not really a Norwich man, for he was born in Wymondham. However, after his family had moved to Norwich, he was orphaned at the age of four and was looked after by the Board of Guardians until he enlisted as a professional soldier fourteen years later, so perhaps Norwich can claim to have been, at least, his foster-mother. Anyway, no such thoughts bothered the minds of the city folk as they prepared to welcome their hero — the man who had been to Buckingham Palace to receive that coveted decoration from the King.

Harry Daniels' pride at the award was somewhat dimmed by the fact that his best friend, who shared in the exploit and also received the V.C., did not survive to share the glory. He was Corporal Cecil ('Tom') Noble, and the pair had struck up a lasting friendship during service in India before the outbreak of war. The *London Gazette*, with characteristic brevity, recorded the award in the following terms:

"For most conspicuous bravery on March 12th 1915, at Neuve Chapelle. When their battalion was impeded in the advance to the attack by the wire entanglements, and subject to a very severe machine gun fire, these two men voluntarily rushed in front and succeeded in cutting the wires. They were both wounded at once, and Corporal Noble has since died of his wounds".

Harry Daniels was described by everybody who knew him as, amongst other things, a man of great modesty. Nevertheless, a persistent newspaperman, patiently waiting by his bedside in the London hospital where he was recovering from his wounds, succeeded in extracting a more detailed account of the action, thus:

"I was instructed by my senior officer to get men to cut away the wire entanglements which were impeding our progress. It had to be done. What could I do? I could not tell men that they had got to go and face what was almost certain death. What I always say is, if there's anything to be done, don't talk about it, but get on with it. I said to my chum, 'Come on, Tom; get some nippers!'

"Together we went forward. Lying in all positions, we cut the wire under a very heavy machine gun fire. After we had been at it for some little time I 'stopped one'; a bullet passed clean through my left thigh. Then I heard Tom making a noise, and I called out, 'What's up, Tom?' Noble faintly replied, 'I've stopped it'. 'Where?' 'In the chest or stomach, old man'. Tom was the coolest and bravest man I ever knew. Although wounded, he pulled himself up and, after cutting some more wire, he fell back exhausted. Again and again he did this until he grew so feeble that he at last sank upon the ground insensible and, soon after, died.

"I saw a shell hole, and crawled along and got into it. But it was not big enough to cover me, so I put my head down into the hole, with my buttocks towards the enemy. It was no laughing matter. There I lay, trying to go to sleep, and wondering whether I should become unconscious. I was thankful enough when darkness came, for I dragged myself to our trenches and safety".

This, then, was the man whom the people of Norwich, in their thousands, turned out to welcome on June 10th 1915. It was very much a two-pronged public relations exercise for, whilst it boosted public morale, there was another hoped-for outcome. As the *Eastern Daily Press* said at the time: "It is not too much to hope that by way of an incidental benefit the admiration kindled in many a youthful breast will have effects agreeable to the recruiting officers".

Harry and his wife duly arrived at Thorpe Station to be met on the platform by the Lord Mayor and his Lady. Then, travelling in the state coaches and with mounted police in attendance, they made their way over Foundry Bridge and along Prince of Wales Road past cheering crowds made larger by the fact that it was early closing day. The Market Place was densely crowded and, as the coaches made their way up Guildhall Hill, a woman dashed from the crowd and presented him with a bouquet of flowers. At the Guildhall, the party was met by the Deputy Lord Mayor and the Town Clerk and, on passing into the Council Chamber, the soldier hero found himself face to face with a cheering throng comprising no less than 9 aldermen, 32 councillors and various representatives of every facet of the city's life.

Then, with the appropriate speeches, Harry was assured of the city's pride in its son and was presented with an illuminated address engrossed on vellum and bearing the Corporate Seal of the Mayor, Aldermen and Citizens of the City of Norwich. He, in reply, spoke in a most accomplished manner. He said all the right things but, being a man of strong convictions, he commented upon two matters which caused him concern. One was "the hundreds of young men still on the streets of Norwich who could, I think, go out and do the same as I have done". The other arose from the fact that his arrival coincided with a strike by tramway workers in support of their claim for payment of a War Bonus. "Suppose we struck for another halfpenny or a penny," he said, "where should we be? We should probably be taken round the corner and shot".

But everything passed off well. Harry had played his part and the people of Norwich were in fine spirit. Then it was off to the Boys' Home in St. Faith's Lane, where he had spent four or five years of his boyhood after the death of his parents. Here there were more speeches, followed by an informal tea with members of the Board of Guardians and an assortment of lady workers. Harry beamed through it all, and his wife, close by his side, bathed in the reflected glow of the adulation being bestowed on him. A friend of mine, now in her nineties but then just a young teenager, witnessed

Civic reception for Harry Daniels at the Guildhall.

Harry and his wife take tea with the Board of Guardians at the Boys' Home.

it all at close quarters, for her father was a member of the Board and she went along, complete with autograph book. At a quiet moment in the proceedings, she approached his table and asked if he would sign his name in it. He quietly flicked through the pages, thought for a while and wrote:

> "I've looked these pages o'er and o'er,
> To see what others said before;
> But ne'er a word has yet been said
> Of Neuve Chapelle and its bloodshed".

Harry was, and still is, her hero.

The following morning he visited his old school at Thorpe Hamlet, where all eyes became rivetted on the famous honour he wore upon his breast. Then he was off to London Street to see the next day's *Eastern Daily Press* being prepared with full reports of his activities.

That evening Harry and his wife, with two friends, went to the Hippodrome for a performance of a revue called 'September Morn'. At the invitation of the proprietors, Messrs Bostock and Fitt, they occupied a private box and, as they entered, the orchestra struck up with 'See the Conquering Hero Comes', accompanied by enthusiastic cheers from the audience. Eventually the lights went down and, after a short pause, the curtain rose. The entire company of the revue was assembled in the background whilst, in front, stood Harry Daniels, still smiling and as self possessed as if he had been bred to the life of the footlights. It was said that his smile never left his face during his entire stay in Norwich. Small wonder that the people of the city dubbed him "the laughing V.C. of Neuve Chapelle".

There can be no disputing the fact that Harry Daniels was a remarkable man. The story of his exploits at Neuve Chapelle could well have occupied several pages of the *Boys' Own Paper*. The story of his life, however, could have filled several complete editions.

He was born on December 13th 1884 in a room above the baker's shop on the edge of Wymondham Market Place, where his father was struggling to support an ever-growing family. Young Harry was the thirteenth child — and there were still three more to come. After a few years the family moved to Norwich, where his father took over a business in Eagle Walk, just off Newmarket Road. Two years later, tragedy struck when his mother died, with six of the family still under the age of 14. Soon afterwards the father died and, though some of the children were in a position to fend for themselves, there were five who were still of very tender years. One of the boys, Joseph, was, for some unaccountable reason, despatched to an orphanage in Bristol; two of the girls, Gertrude and Lily, became inmates of the Girls' Orphanage in Chapel Field Road; Harry and his brother Robert were received into the Boys' Home in St. Faith's Lane under the care of the Board of Guardians. It seemed that four-year-old Harry was suffering the effects of the double thirteen — the thirteenth child, born on the thirteenth of the month.

He attended Thorpe Hamlet School and, when he was old enough, was boarded out at 82 Armes Street, North Heigham, and apprenticed as a carpenter at the Duke's Palace Steam Joinery Works. The routine of this humdrum existence proved too much for his adventurous temperament and, when he was eighteen and with his apprenticeship not completed, he absconded. By the time the authorities caught up with him he had enlisted as a private soldier in the 2nd Battalion of the Rifle Brigade (the Prince Consort's Own).

It was in India that he came into his own. He rapidly achieved the reputation of being a fine all-round athlete, with many trophies to his name, and he was a leading light in the battalion's dramatic club. Steady promotion came his way and, on the outbreak of war, he had achieved the highest non-commissioned rank in the army. On returning to his regiment after recovering from the wounds he suffered at Neuve Chapelle, he was granted a commission and became a second lieutenant. Later, he again distinguished himself in battle and was awarded the Military Cross. When peace returned, he resumed his sporting activities and, in 1920, he represented Britain as a boxer in the Olympic Games in Antwerp. He continued his army career until 1942, when he retired after 39 years' service which had seen him rise to the rank of lieutenant colonel — not a bad record for the little boy who grew up from such humble beginnings.

Harry Daniels never came back to Norwich. He and his wife retired to Leeds, where he managed the Grand Theatre and where he died in 1953 on his 69th birthday.

The last year of my early schooling, before the plunge into a grammar school routine, was spent at St. Mark's School in

Norwich. Coming from the country, I viewed with certain misgivings my first close encounter with city boys, but any such qualms soon proved unjustified. It was to be one of the happiest years of my school life, for St. Mark's was a splendid establishment. Under the headmastership of Edward Snell there was always plenty to occupy our minds, and boredom never reared its head. Even in the classroom, where one's mind might sometimes be inclined to wander, there were two objects which unfailingly attracted my attention.

On one wall, secure in a glass case, was a cricket bat. It was no ordinary bat for on the reverse of the blade it bore, on one side, the signatures of the Norfolk County team and, on the other, those of the West Indians. I never discovered the significance of that bat, but its presence on the wall somehow seemed reassuring.

Facing it from the opposite wall was a photograph of a man wearing the Army uniform of the First World War. Underneath was the inscription:

CORPORAL SIDNEY JAMES DAY, V.C.
Boys of St. Mark's — Remember him.

Sidney Day was, indeed, an Old Boy of the School and he became the second Norwich man to be awarded the Victoria Cross. It was on August 26th 1917 that he performed the gallant deeds which brought him the award, in a manner described in the *London Gazette* in the following words:

"For most conspicuous bravery. Corporal Day was in command of a bombing section detailed to clear a maze of trenches still held by the enemy. This he did, killing two machine gunners and taking four prisoners. On reaching a point where the trench had been levelled, he went alone and bombed his way through to the left in order to gain touch with the neighbouring troops. Immediately on his return to his section a stick bomb fell into a trench occupied by two officers (one badly wounded) and three other ranks. Corporal Day seized the bomb and threw it over the trench, where it immediately exploded. This prompt action undoubtedly saved the lives of those in the trench. He afterwards completed the clearing of the trench and, establishing himself in an advanced position, remained for 66 hours at his post, which came under intense hostile shell and rifle grenade fire. Throughout the whole operations his conduct was an inspiration to all".

69

Sidney Day, the youngest of a family of nine brothers and sisters, was born in 1891 at Morgan's Old Brewery in King Street, where his father was for many years head cellarman. Apart from his attendance at St. Mark's School, he attended the Sunday School of that parish and was also a highly-regarded sergeant in the local Church Lads' Brigade. On leaving school he was apprenticed to Mr. Miller, a butcher on St. Catherine's Plain, and he subsequently took up a situation at Saxmundham, where he was living when war was declared. He wasted little time in answering the country's call to arms and, being in Suffolk, he enlisted in that county's regiment. He spent the next twelve months training at various places in the south of England, being promoted to lance corporal in the process, after which it can justly be said that he had an exceedingly busy war.

In August 1915 he went to France with his battalion, arriving just in time to take part in the battle of Loos. There he underwent an immediate baptism of fire. The battalion got themselves into a very tight corner and his platoon lost contact with the main body. Such was the intensity of the gunfire that, before long, he realised that he was the only uninjured man in the platoon. Nearby, badly wounded, he saw his officer, Lieutenant Stevens. He must be saved at all costs, so Sidney picked him up in his arms and was in the process of carrying him to a place of safety when a bullet from a sniper's rifle made further efforts useless — the lieutenant was dead. No official commendation was forthcoming for his action, but the officer's family recognised his heroism by presenting him with a suitably inscribed cigarette case.

The situation at the time was such that it was three days before Sidney was able to make contact with the main body of his battalion. Then they moved north into Belgium and played their part in the fighting which took place in the area around Ypres in the winter months of 1915.

Some months later it was the battle of Mons which demanded their attention, and it was there, in September 1916, that Sidney had a miraculous escape from death. Mons was a vicious, inhuman engagement and, in the early hours of one fateful morning, he suffered no less than four gunshot wounds in various parts of his body. One bullet struck him directly over the heart but, as luck would have it, he had in his breast pocket two or three notebooks, some postcards and about a dozen field cards. The bullet passed through them all but was deflected in its path, entering his side and coming out at his back. A second bullet struck his groin, a third passed through his thigh and the remaining bullet found its way through his side. Thus wounded and exhausted, he lay in a shell hole from seven o'clock in the morning until nightfall. Then, under cover of darkness, he managed to drag himself three miles to a dressing station, from where he was later brought back to England.

As luck would have it, he found himself installed in the Norfolk War Hospital which had been established at the Mental Hospital at Thorpe. After two months he had recovered sufficiently to be sent to a convalescent home at Wymondham and, early in 1917, he was back across the Channel to join his unit in the bitter fighting around Ypres and Passchendaele. It was there, on the afternoon of Sunday August 26th, that his act of courage earned him the Victoria Cross. The award was not officially announced until mid-October, but Sidney obviously had prior knowledge of it for, in a letter to his parents on September 4th, he wrote:

"In about six weeks' time you will, I hope, be informed of great news, which will make you the proudest parents in Norwich. I am recommended for the coveted honour, the V.C., the first one in this battalion up to the present. Now I know you want to hear all about it, and what I did to get it. Shall be able to tell you more about it when I come home. Am sure it cannot be a greater surprise to you than it has been to me. You cannot imagine how honoured I feel to break the news to you all. Last Sunday week, August 26th, we went over to the attack. Everything went off successful and, thanks to God's mercy and care, I came through untouched. When we got back to our billets my platoon officer, who is a perfect gentleman, broke the news to me. He called me aside and told me that he was very pleased with what I had done in the attack, and was recommending me for a reward. At first, he said, I was in for a M.M., but the captain and himself decided on a D.C.M., but finally the colonel and captain thought me worthy of the Victoria Cross, as he told me personally I thoroughly deserved it, and he hoped I would get it. Well, when my officer told me that, you might have knocked me down with a feather, for little did I dream that I should ever be the one to gain that much-coveted honour. The Colonel congratulated me personally. He came to my billet and said, Corporal, I have come to congratulate you on the splendid work you did last Sunday. I am very proud of you".

It was almost Christmas before Sidney came home on his next leave and, like Harry Daniels before him, he was fêted by the

Civic reception for Sidney Day at the Guildhall.

Sidney Day with his old unit of the Church Lads' Brigade.

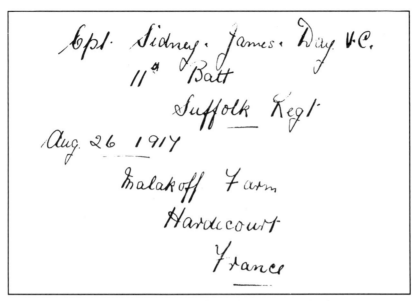

Sidney's inscription in Eddie Codling's autograph book.

citizens of Norwich. The City Council received him at the Guildhall, where the proudest onlookers must surely have been his parents and his soldier brother. The next day, with his sister, he returned to his old school, where they sang patriotic songs and presented him with a clock. Then it was off to St. Mark's Mission Hall in Trafalgar Street for a social evening arranged in his honour by his old company of the Church Lads' Brigade.

All too soon his leave was over and he was back in France to continue the war. Then, on April 10th 1918, his parents received the dreaded news that he had been posted as Missing. All was well, however, for he was in a prisoner-of-war camp, from which he returned after the armistice.

Taking up civilian life once again, he obtained employment with the Electric Light Company and became known to many Norwich folk as he went round wiring their homes for this new form of power. One of them, Eddie Codling, still cherishes the entry in his autograph book inscribed by the local hero.

Sidney Day left his home city in the thirties and went south to Portsmouth, where he married and where he worked in the Dockyard before taking over a shop in the town. He died in Cosham, Hants., in 1959 at the age of 68.

CHAPTER 7

The T.D.L.

I believe I am not alone in thinking that some of the city's old buildings, having outlived the purpose for which they were built, have been too readily demolished rather than adapted to perform some other function. Such undue haste in calling in the bulldozers must surely have led to the loss of many a building which otherwise could have continued to grace the scene for many a long year. The backdrop to the provision market has never seemed quite the same since the demolition men cleared the way for the City Hall, and as for Hay Hill — well, the less said the better.

On the other hand, however, there are many buildings which have survived a change of use and have continued to serve the demands of the folk of both city and county. St. Andrew's Hall, the home of the Dominican Friars nearly seven centuries ago and bought for the city after the Reformation, now houses everything from musical concerts to flea markets. When Mayor Augustine Steward and the City fathers bought the place in 1540, the price paid was £81 and, though the King later demanded a further £152 for the lead on the roof, it must surely represent one of Norwich's biggest bargains. Then there was the Agricultural Hall, opened by Edward, Prince of Wales in 1882, and now forming part of a large television complex. In between times, it has been the scene of a wide variety of events, from circuses and funfairs to trade exhibitions and agricultural shows — and even roller skating.

But for sheer entertainment value few places can challenge the record of the building which, for nearly half a century, stood in St. Andrew's and gloried in the name of the Theatre de Luxe. Most people called it simply the T.D.L. — they couldn't get their tongues round those French words which were creeping into our vocabulary. But, whatever it was called, it had one proud distinction — it was Norwich's first "picture palace". It was in 1910 that history was made, with moving pictures being seen for the first time and, with the coming of the talkies, the T.D.L. became the mecca for the masses. For 47 years it catered for lovers of "a night at the flicks", particularly those whose interest lay in cowboy

"THÉATRE DE LUXE"

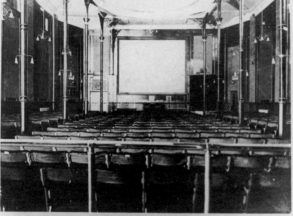

St ANDREWS NORWICH.
Delightful Music.

PICK OF THE PICTURES.

CONSTANT CHANGE OF PROGRAMME.

CONTINUOUS PERFORMANCE 2 TILL 10·30

Popular 3D & 6D prices

pictures, for that was the de Luxe's speciality. Yet those 47 years were little more than a chapter in the history of the building for, when that modern miracle arrived in Norwich, the old place had already been providing the people of the city with entertainment and instruction for nearly eighty years.

It was in the early 1830s that the building had first opened its doors to the public, announcing itself as the Royal Bazaar — the regal prefix probably being not unconnected with the fact that the foundation stone was laid on September 8th 1831, the coronation day of William IV. There seems to be little record of what went on inside the bazaar, though it is said that a corn curer did good business, as did various purveyors of pills and potions. Before long, however, the style of the place changed and, with displays of engineering models and daily scientific lectures, it became known as the Lecture Hall.

One of the great attractions on its many visits to Norwich was Poole's Diorama, which delighted its audiences with pictures of faraway places. Magic lantern shows were commonplace, but the diorama gave them a greater sense of realism with the cunning use of a variable lighting system which, when directed at the back of the screen, appeared to bring everything to life. It was particularly effective in portraying such things as the flickering lanterns in a Chinese street scene or the storm-tossed waters of the Bay of Biscay. To be correct, the full title of the entertainment was "Poole's Diorama WITH EFFECTS", the effects being provided by a little old man sitting at the back with a drum and a bugle. Whatever picture came up on the screen, he could be relied upon to use either instrument — and sometimes both — to provide an added dimension to the performance.

The scope of the attractions offered at the Hall was forever widening, but it would seem that the type of exhibition in which the citizens of Norwich showed the most enthusiastic, if morbid, interest was the freaks of nature which regularly went the rounds. There was Captain Bates, an American heavyweight tipping the scales at 34 stones, and the Chinese giant called Chang, standing nine feet tall in his fancy shoes. Challenging them in size was Mariedl, the 27-year-old Tyrolean Giantess who weighed 360 pounds and whose daily diet was said to include 14 pounds of cereals and vegetables, two quarts of Oxo and a quart of milk. So great was her success that she returned to the city in 1907 to appear twice nightly at the Hippodrome.

As a contrast, there came the mysteriously-named Madame Ghio, who was quite normal in height and weight but who sported a most luxurious beard which would have done credit to any man. But perhaps the most sensational of all was a mulatto woman by the name of Christine Miller. Mulattos — the product of a union between a European and a negro — were something of a rarity in Norwich at that time. The fact that this one had two heads made her appearance even more sensational — especially when she sang a duet with herself! Presumably it was all done with mirrors.

This was certainly the case with "The Living Wonder", the young girl whose appearance almost brought the house down in more ways than one. She was introduced by a sword-carrying barker who, standing before a wardrobe-like cabinet, whetted the audience's appetite with the information that "she can talk but she cannot walk". Then, having roused his audience to a state of eager anticipation, he flung open the door of the cabinet to reveal the girl — or, at least, part of her, for there was nothing below the waist! To prove that there was no deception he swung his sword from side to side where her legs should have been, and then he called on her to recite a poem, followed by a little snatch of a song. The audience were spellbound, for it was quite true what the man had said — she could talk, but she certainly couldn't walk without any legs. But it was unfortunate for the girl that, amongst the crowd of onlookers, there happened to be two young seafaring gentlemen who had seen a similar exhibition in some Far Eastern port. They advanced towards the cabinet and, in the scuffle that ensued, one of the sides collapsed, revealing the young girl, complete with legs, standing at the side. She had not been in the cabinet at all — it had been merely her reflection. In his introductory speech, the barker had said nothing about her ability to run but, when last seen, she was sprinting down St. Andrew's with a horde of young lads in hot pursuit.

By 1872 the Lecture Hall, suitably refurbished, had become the Victoria Hall and had begun to attract performers of a higher standard. Indeed, many famous artistes came from London to perform there, among them George Grossmith and the Great Vance. Then, in 1880, the D'Oyly Carte Opera Company gave the first performance in Norwich of H.M.S. Pinafore. Classical musicians proved highly popular and, in 1906, the Hall was full for a recital by Michael Zacharewitsch, the Russian-born violinist who had been hailed by Tschaikovsky as the greatest living

Michael Zacharewitsch,

Said by Tschaikowsky to be the Greatest Living Violinist.

Victoria Rooms, Norwich, Jan. 25th, 1906.

The Theatre de Luxe shortly before its closure in 1957.

exponent of that instrument and who later became a naturalised British subject.

But it was the year 1910 which saw the Victoria Hall change its name yet again and start its new life as the Theatre de Luxe. Then, for nearly half a century, it drew the crowds to witness the modern miracle of motion pictures. In those early days, of course, there was neither sound nor colour, and most of the films were "shorts", but the T.D.L. always gave its patrons their money's-worth. The first programme consisted of seven such films, with as wide a diversity of subject as the titles suggest: *The Dancing Girl of Bute, Frankfort, The Corsican's Revenge, Ma Goes To Work, The Airship Destroyer, Generous Rivals* and *Dispensing With a Barber.* And all that for 3d. or 6d., with children half price.

In the years that followed, many new cinemas arrived on the scene. Indeed, at one time Norwich could have been described as suffering from a surfeit of riches in that respect, many of them far more luxurious than the Theatre de Luxe. The old place never became one of the city's top cinemas, but it was homely and it gave its faithful patrons what they wanted, and they loved it for that. When they referred to it as "The Fleapit", they were using the phrase as a term of endearment rather than in any critical sense. If they wanted cowboy films, that was what the management gave them, and there was rarely a week when some western hero or other was not riding the range within those walls in St. Andrew's.

But then came television and, like so many other cinemas, the T.D.L. found its audiences dwindling. The end came with the last performance on February 11th 1957. It was the end of an era spanning 126 years during which the old building, in its various guises, had entertained and informed the people of the city. It was a sad night, made even sadder by the loutish behaviour of a band of hooligans who saw fit to smash seats and doors and hurl the resultant debris through the screen before themselves being manhandled out by hastily-called police. But the memories remain of that modest little picture-house — unpretentious but dearly loved.

CHAPTER 8

Mysterious Norfolk.

It seems natural that Norfolk, with its many historical associations and its wealth of ancient buildings, should play host to a goodly assortment of ghostly manifestations and mysteries. Unfortunately, some of the better-known examples have been badly treated over the years by a succession of writers who have embellished the stories with features which were not originally present. The ghosts have been dragged out of the cupboard and, not content with simple resuscitation, eager scribes have invented details which have destroyed not only their authenticity but also the very features which made them typically Norfolk.

Old Shuck is one of the more glaring examples of such treatment. This placid creature, searching the byways of Norfolk since 1709 for his shipwrecked master, has become a vicious fiend. With huge red eyes and evil intent he is now nothing more than the ghostly black dog of Celtic legend.

It is the same with Sir Thomas Boleyn who, on May 19th every year, drives a coach from Blickling in a frantic attempt to cross eleven bridges before dawn. The story is a good one, but we are now told that poor Sir Thomas and his four horses are all headless — simply a replica of the vast array of headless horsemen who charge around country roads in almost every corner of the kingdom.

But there are still many strange mysteries and ghostly apparitions whose memories remain unsullied and who retain the charm of being truly Norfolk in character. There is, for instance, the lavender-scented ghost who comforts the sick at the Old Rectory at Snetterton. This benevolent spirit is an elderly, mob-capped woman who appears when the occupants of the house are in pain or cannot sleep. She seems to be particularly drawn towards sick children, bringing with her a feeling of warmth and such a strong scent of lavender that the fragrance rapidly fills the room. A few years ago, a senior member of the family living at the house proposed that steps should be taken to have the ghost exorcised. Fortunately, the suggestion was met with cries of protest and near-mutiny in the family, and the perfumed comforter remains in residence.

Then there are Ann and Jacob, the mother and son who ask no more than to be allowed to dwell in peace at the 18th-century White Horse Inn at Wymondham. The unfortunate couple perished in a fire at the inn many years ago and, ever since then, their spirits have shared the premises with successive hosts and their customers. They have long had the reputation of being a friendly couple — but that can change when they are upset! Quite recently, a new manager was installed at the White Horse and, on hearing from his patrons the story of Ann and Jacob, he ridiculed the suggestion. Then, in order to register his disbelief, he went to the extreme length of installing an inflatable plastic skeleton in the large fireplace. It was then that things began to happen.

Light fittings in the bar moved from one place to another. The manager's cigarettes and lighter disappeared from a table and were never seen again. The area around the fireplace became so incredibly cold and spooky that even the cat would give it a wide berth. The sliding door between the bar and the staircase noisily opened and closed without the help of a human hand. And even the barrels in the cellar, kept in a certain order by the manager, mysteriously moved themselves around.

Only when the manager departed, taking with him the plastic skeleton, did peace return to the White Horse.

Deep in the heart of the Norfolk countryside, on the eastern fringe of Breckland, stands Breckles Hall, a fine Elizabethan manor house which, for five centuries, was the seat of successive lords of the manor. It boasts a panelled hall and three octagonal staircases, with the added embellishment of stained glass portraying the coats of arms of its earlier occupiers. It is one of those houses which, if they are not haunted, jolly well ought to be, and even some of its earlier occupants were the very stuff of which ghost stories are made. It was a favourite hiding place of banished priests during the reign of the Virgin Queen; it was the home of an eccentric woman who insisted on being buried in an upright position; and rumour has it that two of its earlier owners committed suicide. A place like that would hardly be complete without a ghost or two.

But, haunted or not, it was at this house, a couple of centuries ago, that a phantom coach called and brought an untimely end to

George Mace. George Mace was a Watton man who, like the owls, was usually active only at night and who, again like the owls, went about his business in the local game coverts. Mace was a strange character with a mysterious power over the men with whom he associated and, if there was a bit of law-breaking to be done, he was the man to whom they all turned for leadership.

On the night in question, he and a band of similar felons gathered in a plantation near Breckles Hall with the intention of engaging in a night's poaching in the grounds of the Hall and in the nearby coverts of Lord Walsingham's Merton estate. In order that the night's haul might be as large as possible, it was decided that they would split into a number of smaller groups and, at the end of the proceedings, they would all meet at a chosen spot at the rear of Breckles Hall and there "settle up before the moon went down".

It was a very successful night for the poachers, and there was great excitement as they later gathered at the chosen rendezvous for the "settling up". Only one thing cast a cloud over the proceedings — there was no sign of their mysterious leader. They waited impatiently, peering through the moonlight in all directions and listening intently for the slightest sound, but still George Mace failed to appear. Slowly the moon sank towards the horizon with not so much as a sound to break the stillness of the night.

Then, as darkness took over the scene, the silence was suddenly shattered by the sound of carriage wheels and, within minutes, the flashing of coach lamps could be seen through the stained glass windows of the old Hall. So bright, indeed, was the light that "the very coats of arms were painted on the hoar frost" down by the feet of the watching men. On reaching the door of the Hall, the coach stopped, its door opened and almost immediately slammed shut again. Then there was utter darkness. The lamps went out and the coach vanished into thin air without a sound.

The men stood as if rooted to the spot by what had appeared before them. Then, as panic took over their senses, they fled the scene and sought the sanctuary of their respective homes. What thoughts went through their minds during the remainder of that long night can only be imagined. But what happened as the first rays of daylight filtered over the countryside must surely have brought a vow that never again would they keep a midnight vigil in the neighbourhood of Breckles Hall. For there, on the front step, lay the body of George Mace with "not a mark on his body; not a stain upon his garments — just his eyes staring glassily, stiff and cold!"

Lest it be thought that the lady of Breckles Hall who insisted on being buried standing up was somewhat eccentric, it should be said that, compared with John Balls of Happisburgh, she was almost mundanely conventional. He, for reasons which history neglects to disclose, elected to go to his grave with a poker at his feet and a fistful of plum cake in either hand. There were those in the village who said that the presence of the poker was to enable him to defend himself against the keeper of the nether regions which surely must be his final destination. Others claimed that it would keep the fires burning while he and the devil consumed the cake together.

Such unkind statements concerning the deceased may seem rather heartless, but they were nevertheless justified, for it is generally accepted that, at a conservative reckoning, he was responsible for the death by arsenical poisoning of at least sixteen residents of the parish of Happisburgh — and most of them were members of his own family! Strangely enough, the Balls family was said to be a happy and united one, and Jonathan was held in high esteem as a devoted husband and grandfather. Within a short distance of the cottage in which he lived with his wife Elizabeth there dwelt their three married daughters — Mesdames Pestle, Green and Peggs — together with their numerous offspring. The only thing which cast a shadow over the contentment of their lives was that, between the years 1836 and 1845, two little Pestles, seven young Greens, three small Peggs and Grandma Balls all died — and each time the symptoms were identical. On every occasion, a child would visit the Grandfather, or vice versa, and then would come the sudden vomiting and the child would be dead.

It seems odd that no questions were ever asked and that there was never an inquest. Even the Vicar, Mr. Burch, remained strangely unquestioning throughout all his steady repetitions of the burial service. A cloud of fear hung over the village and suspicion was rife, but there were two reasons why the parishioners kept their silence. Firstly, there was the belief among some that it was purely a family matter — "that in't northing ter dew wi' me". Then there were those who feared that, should they make an accusation against Balls, they might be next on his list. Indeed, there was one such man, Nye by name, who went so far as to express his fears in public and drew forth the wrath of the accused. The quarrel was later reconciled over a pint of ale — handed to Nye by Balls, of course. Within twenty four hours Nye had breathed his last!

The real cause of all the trouble was that Jonathan Balls was unemployed — indeed, he was unemployable. His true vocation had been arson and he only changed to murder when this became too dangerous, for it was a time when arson was still a hanging offence. He was a most inefficient fire-raiser and, on one occasion, was arrested and charged but escaped the supreme penalty solely because of lack of evidence. After one conflagration he was even prepared to swear false witness to incriminate an innocent man and thereby collect the £300 reward relating to one of his own fires.

Thus it was that Balls fell back on his daughters for his keep. However, as the size of their families steadily increased, so they found it ever more difficult to fulfil their duties to the old man. Hence, he reluctantly decided that there was only one solution — there must be a cull. The numbers must be reduced to a level which would permit his daughters to continue to maintain him. So, one by one, twelve of the children were removed, together with several members of the adult population.

Then, in 1846, Balls met his death, and it seems only fitting that he should die in the same manner as his victims and at his own hands. Any other ending would somehow have been lacking in justice. Yet, even then, there was no inquiry and no post mortem. They took him to his burial place, and there they laid him to rest with a poker at his feet and a fistful of fruit cake in each hand.

Only when he was safely put away did the cloud of suspicion begin to lift from the village. Then, no longer having to face the man they accused, the parishioners made their feelings known to such a degree that officialdom finally had to bow to the demand for an investigation. The County Coroner, Mr. Pilgrim, somewhat reluctantly put the wheels in motion and the grim task of exhumation began. In due course it was officially conceded that the cause of death in each case was arsenical poisoning. Indeed, the medical evidence was that the amount of arsenic found in the graves was sufficient to poison every person in the parish!

Mr. Pilgrim listened to all the information put before him, but hard evidence was flooded by a storm of accusation and suspicion. He could do no more than direct the jury to bring in an open verdict for, though murder had undoubtedly been done and suspicion pointed at Balls, there was no proof "beyond reasonable doubt", as the law required. So, in death as in life, lack of evidence enabled Jonathan Balls to escape the vengeance of the law, and he went to his grave an innocent man.

But who can tell why he wanted to take the poker and the plum cake with him?

And who, indeed, can explain the mysterious happenings which drew a London woman to a ghostly confrontation in Snettisham church?

There are several things about the Snettisham Ghost which tend to make it unique amongst the spectral apparitions of Norfolk. Most significant of all is the fact that it can claim to be a genuinely true ghost story, for every detail was investigated and authenticated by the Society for Psychical Research.

The sequence of events began when, in October 1893, a certain Mrs. Goodeve left her London home and travelled down to the West Country to spend a few days with her friends, Mr. and Mrs. Ackland, on the outskirts of Bristol. There, at number 5 Rodney Place, Clifton, it was just a happy reunion with not the slightest indication of the drama which was about to unfold. After all, they were all worldly people, not given to fanciful imaginations about such things as spiritual visitors from another world. Mrs. Goodeve, indeed, was "a widow lady moving in good society, with grown-up children and known to many people as a cheerful, capable, active woman who had seen much of the world".

It was during the night of October 8th that the first act of the drama took place. Mrs. Goodeve was fast asleep in her bed when, in the silence of the night, she suddenly woke with a start to find the figure of a woman leaning over her. The woman's face, sad and emaciated yet with a kindly expression, was wrapped in some kind of cloth resembling a shawl. Mrs. Goodeve looked up at the face with some degree of surprise but with no feeling of fear, and then the visitor spoke.

"Follow me", she said.

Puzzled but intrigued, Mrs. Goodeve rose from her bed and, taking a candle to light her way, followed her ghostly visitor through into the drawing room. There, the spirit went to the far end of the room and, turning, uttered just one word — "Tomorrow" — and then promptly vanished. Mrs. Goodeve returned to her bedroom and immediately fell back into a deep sleep.

The next morning, Mrs. Goodeve told the story of her nocturnal visitor to her hosts and also to a neighbour, a certain Dr. Marshall. He immediately identified the spirit as being that of the late Mrs. Seagrim, whom he had earlier tended and who had been in the habit of wrapping her head in an Indian shawl in an effort to relieve the pain of neuralgia from which she suffered.

On the following night Mrs. Goodeve was again awakened from her sleep by the same apparition, who said, "I have come. Listen to what I have to say". Poor Mrs. Goodeve was mystified. "Am I dreaming," she said, "or is this really true?"

"If you doubt me", said the visitor, "you will find that I was married on the 26th of September 1860. (Mrs. Goodeve was later to verify with Dr. Marshall that that was indeed the date on which the late Mrs. Seagrim had been married in India to an army major). "I have somebody with me", continued the apparition. "We have a task for you to perform".

It was at this point that Mrs. Goodeve became aware of a second figure — that of a man who declared himself to be "Henry Barnard, buried in Snettisham churchyard". This was the first time she had ever heard of Snettisham, and she had no idea of its location. The man proceeded to give her details of the task he wished her to perform. He began by telling her the dates of his marriage and death, which she could verify in the church register at Snettisham. She was then required to take a white rose from his grave and send it to Dr. Marshall. Then she was to enter the church at 1-15 the next morning and go to the south-west corner of the south aisle to the tomb of a certain Robert Cobb, who had died on May 15th 1743. There she would receive the final details of her task.

Mrs. Goodeve was, to say the least, intrigued and her sense of wonderment was further heightened by three predictions which the spirit of Henry Barnard proceeded to make concerning her trip to Snettisham. Firstly, he said, the outgoing half of her railway ticket would not be taken from her; then she would obtain help from "a dark man" who would recognise her description of the speaker; and, finally, she would find lodgings at the home of a woman whose child, having died from drowning, was buried in the same churchyard.

As the speaker came to the end of his discourse, Mrs. Goodeve became aware of the presence of yet another ghostly figure, a man whose identity was not revealed to her. But, she said, he was obviously greatly troubled, "his face so full of misery that I could hardly bear to look upon it".

After the night's encounter, Mrs. Goodeve could hardly wait to get back to London and make preparations for a visit to Snettisham. Enquiries at the Post Office revealed the location of the village and, on the following Saturday, she boarded the train for her trip to North Norfolk. During the hours that followed, all three of her visitor's predictions came true. The outward half of her ticket was not collected and, on enquiring of the porter as to where she might obtain lodgings, she was directed to the home of John Bishop, the parish clerk. It was immediately apparent to her that he was the "dark man" and, furthermore, he readily recognised her description of her nocturnal visitor as being Henry Barnard, the late owner of Cobb Hall. Then, in conversation with John Bishop's wife, she was told that their daughter, having met with death by drowning, had been interred in Snettisham churchyard.

The next day being Sunday, Mrs. Goodeve attended morning service at the church and took the opportunity of inspecting the register to verify the facts given to her by the apparition of Henry Barnard. Then she made arrangements with John Bishop to be admitted to the church at about one o'clock the next morning and to be locked in for half an hour. Once inside, she waited by the tomb of Robert Cobb and, in due course, she received the final part of the message, which she was to deliver to Barnard's only surviving daughter at Cobb Hall. With it, she was to take another white rose from Henry Barnard's grave, and then her task would be complete.

And what was the message? We shall never know, for that was the only part of this intriguing story which Mrs. Goodeve steadfastly refused to reveal. John Bishop spoke of hearing voices while he waited outside the church, but they were not sufficiently audible for him to hear what was said. Mrs. Goodeve kept her secret to the last, so we will never solve the mystery of the force which brought together such a varied collection of spirits in their nocturnal visitations. Nor will we know why it was that a London woman, on holiday in Bristol, should have been chosen as the central figure in binding together such a web of ghostly intrigue.

CHAPTER 9

The Age of the Train.

The arrival in Norfolk of the railways brought a great change into the lives of many people who, all over the county, began to avail themselves of the increased mobility offered by the new means of transpo.t. But travelling had never been much of an obsession with most Norfolk countryfolk, who knew what legs were for and used them to the full. In any case, most of them rarely went further than the nearest town on market day and, for the housewife, there was usually the chance of a lift on the carrier's cart.

In the case of longer journeys there was transport of a slightly more luxurious nature for those who had the need and, indeed, the financial means to make use of it. All over the county the turnpikes and some of the lesser roads echoed to the sound of horses' hooves and carriage wheels as the more affluent members of society travelled for reasons of business or pleasure. From the King's Arms at North Walsham, with two hundred horses in his stables and paddocks, Robert Walpole Palmer ran a fleet of horse buses to the increasingly fashionable coastal resorts of Cromer, Sheringham, Mundesley and Overstrand. On a grander and more exciting scale, there was the "Express" Coach which, in the middle of the last century, regularly travelled between Cromer and Norwich. Driven by Mad Wyndham of Felbrigg, it left Cromer at 8 o'clock in the morning and reached the Black Boys Hotel at Aylsham at nine for a change of horses. The steady pace of eight miles per hour was then maintained all the way to Norwich, enabling passengers to catch the ten forty-five train for London. At the same time, William Cooper, the renowned North Walsham coachman, was taking the "Pilot" coach through the Norfolk countryside until the fateful day when, coming down the hill past Captain's Pond at Westwick, the coach overturned and he was killed.

But the most renowned coach of all must surely have been the "Lobster", the brainchild of Thomas Cook of Sennowe Park at Guist. Throughout the summer months, the "Lobster" made the journey from Cromer to Norwich and back, calling at Roughton,

The Lobster Coach leaving the Maid's Head, Norwich for Cromer.

A change of horses at the Black Boys Hotel, Aylsham.

Aylsham and St. Faith's in an operation which demanded twenty horses and a staff of thirty-five ostlers and grooms. That great horseman of yesteryear, Captain T. W. Palmer, writing in Brian Vesey-Fitzgerald's *Book of the Horse,* recalled the London firm of Miltons in Park Lane as being the leading horse dealers at that time. "And it was they", he wrote, "who in 1907 horsed the 'Lobster' coach from Cromer to Norwich. It was put on by the late Mr. Thomas Cook of Sennowe and was magnificently done, with four changes for the 22 miles. As a youngster in my teens I took it through many times, and I shall never forget the team of bays, only 15.2 hands, which did the Aylsham to St. Faith's journey of 7 miles each way, this being the best road team I have ever handled".

The spectacle of those splendid horses careering through the Norfolk countryside must surely have been blood-stirring, but their supremacy was soon to be challenged and finally destroyed by the iron horses of the steam age.

There can be little doubt that the coming of the railways had a profound effect on the physical face of Norfolk. Firstly, there were the environmental repercussions as the raw gash of metal tracks spread relentlessly through the county. There were many who resented this carving up of the countryside, just as there are those today who deplore the spread of concrete motorways which, themselves, must surely become obsolete in the not-too-distant future. Then there was the transformation of many of the places which suddenly found themselves physically linked with the rest of the country. Cromer and Sheringham gave up being just sleepy little fishing villages, and Yarmouth plunged headlong into the quest for recognition as a major seaside holiday resort. But one of the most amazing transformations must surely have been that which took place at the sleepy little parish of Melton Constable.

In 1831 Melton had boasted just 114 inhabitants; ten years later, with several families having emigrated to America, that figure had dropped to a mere 75. But, long before the end of the century, the parish of Melton-Constable-with-Burgh-Parva had seen its population soar past the thousand mark — and it had all been brought about by those puffing engines with their mustard-yellow livery and their top-hat chimneys.

It was the Eastern and Midland Company who had laid the lines, later giving way to the Midland and Great Northern Joint Railway. Almost before they knew what was happening, the peaceful folk of Melton Constable found that they had become one of the most important of the county's railway junctions, with direct routes to King's Lynn, Norwich, Yarmouth and Cromer. But it was what came next that caused the population explosion.

The laying of the lines had not presented too much of a problem from the point of view of available labour. Much of the work was carried out by itinerant navvies, supplemented by local agricultural workers who willingly gave up their twelve-shillings-a-week jobs on the land in favour of the eighteen shillings which the railway company offered. With no mechanical aids, it was hard work digging out the tracks, taking away vast quantities of earth in tip-carts and depositing it in the more low-lying areas, but they were glad enough of that extra six shillings.

It was only when the decision was made to convert Melton Constable into a kind of minature Crewe that the problem of labour arose, for skilled men were required to staff the extensive repair shops and the permanent way depot which arose on the previously unpopulated area of Burgh Parva. To meet this need, entire families were brought in from Derby and the Midlands, and the Company built 56 terraced houses to accommodate them. The Railway Institute was opened in 1896 and enlarged in 1912 for the use of the employees, offering reading and billiard rooms, dining and coffee rooms, a library of 3,000 volumes and a large hall for public meetings and entertainments. The Parish Council even leased nine acres of land from Lord Hastings for use as a recreation ground.

Melton Constable had suddenly become a place of some importance. But it had also become what I have always regarded as the most untypical of all Norfolk villages, thus proving — if such proof were needed — that a true Norfolk village cannot be created overnight.

But Melton Constable flourished until, in more recent years, the bubble burst and the railways fell out of favour. One by one the lines were closed and eventually Melton found itself no longer a part of the country's railway system. The army of mechanics left the repair sheds and the "Melton Buzzer", which had rung out for miles around to summon them to work, fell silent.

One thing which stands out in one's memories of the railways in the days of independence is the pride of the men who kept them running. Whether it was the station, the rolling stock or the Company, they all reckoned theirs was best, and there were always

Railway Fitting Shop at Melton Constable.

The Railway Company's houses at Melton Constable.

inspectors travelling on passenger trains to keep them on their toes. The result was that railway stations were bright and cheerful places, with well-tended flower beds, polite porters and, in cold weather, a blazing coal fire in the waiting room. Wilfred Coleman, who spent most of his working life on the railways in the Wymondham and Hardingham areas, is a living example of that pride as, after a quarter of a century of retirement, he still proudly wears the watch he received after 45 years' service. Wilfred left school at the age of 13 and became yard boy for a local landowner, working a 60-hour week for a wage of 3s. 6d. He later left that post and went to work in a similar capacity at Silfield Lodge, where the owner offered him a shilling more, but this was to end when he reached the age of 16, for it then became necessary for him to have a weekly insurance stamp. The stamp cost sevenpence, of which Wilfred would have to pay threepence, but his employer told him in no uncertain terms, "I don't want to pay for a stamp — I'll get another boy". Thus it was that, in 1916, Wilfred got a job as a lad porter with the Great Eastern Railway Company which, seven years later, was to become part of the London and North Eastern Railway Company.

Wilfred readily recalls the day when he received his first uniform, and I could sense the feeling of pride as he described it to me. It was made of green cord material with a number on each side of the collar — 229 was his number. There was a sleeved waistcoat with the number on the sleeve and, he said, "the trousers had flaps, not flies — like a sailor's bell-bottoms". Porters were given a new suit every three years and, though the old one had to be returned, Wilfred soon learned the dodge by which it could be retained. A certain train would arrive and the old suit had to be thrown in through an open window. However, if the window on the other side was also open, the suit could be thrown straight through to the other platform, to be retrieved later. It seems this ploy was very successful until one occasion when, on going on his retrieval mission, Wilfred realised that a goods train had been standing against the other platform. His suit had landed in one of its wagons, and he watched in anguish as it sped off to some unknown destination.

Before the Great War, a porter worked a 12-hour day for fifteen shillings a week although, in 1919, the hours were reduced to eight. Signalmen were more highly paid but, unlike the porters, they were unable to earn tips for services rendered to the travelling public. This was a great source of income and there were many porters who were better off at the end of the week than the signalmen. There was inevitably a certain amount of friendly enmity between the two grades of workers, as is evidenced by a conversation amongst a group of porters, overheard by the stationmaster.

"I don't know why they issue signalmen with trousers", said one of the porters. "You can only see their top half".

There was no denying this statement, and it was even more relevant in the case of Jim Mulley, one of the signalmen, who was exceedingly short in stature. Indeed, so short was he that he had to stand on a stool to get a full view out of the window and, when he was walking about in the signal box, all that was visible from ground level was his little head bobbing about.

"We could save even more on Jim", chipped in the station master. "All he needs is the hat".

In his early years at Wymondham, young Wilfred had a variety of tasks to perform. One which evokes the very spirit of the age was that of lighting the gas lamps in the carriages of the train which arrived just as dusk was falling. This involved running along the roofs of the carriages, lifting the little lid which each compartment had and lighting each gas mantle in turn with his oil-burning torch. Only when the task had been completed would the train continue its journey. At least, that was what normally happened, but there was one occasion when, for reasons unknown, the driver set his locomotive in motion with Wilfred still busy on the carriage roof. Only by hastily jumping clear did he escape being swept from his perch by the footbridge at the end of the platform.

Another of Wilfred's tasks was to take the mailbags from a horse-drawn vehicle which made a nightly trip from Long Stratton, calling at a number of village post offices on the way. Then there was the matter of "the box". This was a metal container which travelled along the branch lines on a certain train each weekday and into which each stationmaster would place the previous day's takings. It was constructed in such a way that the packets of cash could readily be deposited within, but nothing could be removed until the box reached London, where the key was kept. Wilfred had mixed feelings about the task of transferring the box from the branch line trains to the London express. There was a feeling of pride that he should be entrusted with such an important duty, but there was also the realisation that, while he was thus engaged, his colleagues were busily collecting tips by carrying passengers' luggage.

Wymondham, at that time, was the centre of one of the most thriving farming communities in the county and it sometimes seemed that there were more animals than people travelling by rail. This was particularly the case on Saturdays, with large numbers making the journey to Trowse on their way to Norwich Cattle Market. During his 12-hour night shift, one of Wilfred's duties was to go round to the homes of Dick Bunn, the goods foreman, and Mr. Alcock, the shunt horse driver, to knock them up for a 4 a.m. start.

With so many animals there were bound to be problems. Young horses, encountering the mysteries of rail travel for the first time, were inclined to be fractious, and many a man went home at the end of the day suffering from the effects of a well-directed hoof. In such cases, an older horse which had been through it all before was usually loaded first — once he was on board, the others would meekly follow.

But the biggest troublemakers were the goats, for they were a law unto themselves. Each one had its own individual lead to facilitate movement, but the big problem arose over the destination label which had to be fixed to every animal. With cattle and horses it was just a question of sticking the label on the animals back but, as is well known, goats will eat anything they can get their teeth into. The problem was solved by putting each goat's label on the only place he could not reach — the top of his head. Even so, there was one occasion when even this tactic proved fallible. The station foreman, the appropriately-named George Kidd, was never separated from his pipe, which he lit from a gas jet. On the day in question he was emerging from his office when a stray piece of paper blew to his feet and, without thinking, he proceeded to light his pipe with it. Then, too late, he realised that it was the destination label of some forlorn goat. It seems that confusion reigned when it became apparent that nobody remembered the goat's destination, but history fails to record the final outcome.

The world of the railways in those earlier days was so full of characters and incidents that any novelist would surely find among them a ready-made, true-to-life story just waiting to be written. There was, for instance, the occasion when Wilfred was sent to Strayground level crossing to relieve the regular crossing keeper

Railway staff at Wymondham, 1906.

Shunting horses at Wymondham.

while he had a day off. The roads were quieter places in those days, and Wilfred was called upon to open the gates just once — for the mole-catcher on his way to Silfield on his tricycle.

Then there was the stationmaster at Ryburgh with his passion for the game of bowls. There was a green quite near the station and he would frequently pop across for a game. Before going, however, he would instruct Wilfred to go across to the green some time later, taking with him a telegraph form bearing some kind of cryptic message. The content of the message was of no importance — anything would do. Wilfred would do this and the stationmaster, taking off his spectacles, would give the message his earnest attention. Then, his course of action would depend entirely upon the state of the game in which he was involved. If he was winning, he would say, "Thank you, Coleman. Lay it on my desk"; if he was losing, however, it was "Oh dear! Oh dear! Will somebody take my woods, please. I'm needed at the station".

One of the great traditions which arose during the real age of the train was the railway excursion. The companies, well aware that the cost of running a train fully packed with passengers was no greater than a sparsely occupied one, offered tempting reductions for organised parties. The public, for their part, eagerly accepted the chance of a cheap day out, be it for some special occasion or, in many cases, simply an escape from the drudgery of their drab working week.

It was Norfolk's own Thomas Cook who pioneered this new form of leisure activity by organising a "temperance excursion" from Leicester to Loughborough in 1841. In 1853, Methodists from Diss travelled in a body to Yarmouth on the first of what proved to be a 60-year series of annual trips. It took the coming of the Great War to put a stop to the tradition, by which time the size of the party had risen to 1500. In 1897, not to be outdone, Salvationists from Cromer and Sheringham joined the massive crowd of their fellows who descended on London for the Salvation Army's 32nd anniversary gathering at the Crystal Palace.

But it was the Works Outing which was probably the most popular form of excursion, with workmates becoming playmates for a day and the bosses often joining the party. In 1862, Colman's of Norwich took 500 of their staff from Thorpe Station to visit the International Exhibition in London. The reaction of the workers to their visit to the big city was somewhat mixed, as Jeremiah James

Colman recorded in a letter to his sister. They were full of enthusiasm in proclaiming their enjoyment of the trip, but unimpressed with London, which they considered a very dirty place. "Furthermore", continued Jeremiah, "they did not fancy the people they saw, and one said he did not see a decently fat man all the time he was there".

The traffic was not all one way for, while local folk were seizing the opportunity to visit faraway places, excursionists from far afield were travelling in to discover the delights of Norfolk. On June 16th 1893 the population of Yarmouth exploded for a day with the arrival of 8,000 Bass Brewery workers from Burton-on-Trent. Well over two hundred carriages were needed to bring in this massive party, and two miles of sidings were required to park the trains while the visitors were sampling the pleasures of the town. The excursion was organised with meticulous care, the workers having received prior details of what treats lay in store for them, together with the assurance that "the Great Eastern is the MOST PUNCTUAL line in the kingdom". They were also exhorted to remember the honour of the firm for which they worked. "May I", said the director, "especially beg of all persons to be quiet and orderly on the journeys, on the steamers, at the various places of amusement, in the streets, and generally throughout the day. It should be remembered that this is our first visit to Great Yarmouth; let it therefore be said that Bass & Co employees know how to behave themselves and that all return home perfectly orderly and sober". The workers must have heeded his plea, for the Bass Excursion to Yarmouth became an annual event over many years, to the mutual delight of both the visitors and the traders of the town.

Thus grew the tradition of the railway excursion, reaching its peak in the twenties and thirties and even surviving the austerity of the late forties. Yet the innocent happiness which it brought with it did not take root without a degree of early opposition. The more religious members of society declared that a Sunday excursion was a railway ticket to Hell. Regular rail travellers expressed the fear that their accustomed style would be "compromised by working class usage". But, all around the rail network, day trippers were packing themselves into the carriages in their hundreds, taking with them — in the absence of dining cars — massive quantities of sausage rolls and sandwiches to sustain them on the journey. Then there was the community singing for most of the journey there,

Bass Brewery employees arriving at Yarmouth, 1909.

Boys of the Paston School leaving North Walsham on the first stage of an excursion to Belgium, 1935.

Employees of the Briton Brush Company leaving Wymondham on their annual outing.

with a repeat performance on the return trip until, one by one, they fell asleep from sheer exhaustion.

Steadily, however, a rapid expansion in motor coach travel, coupled with the new freedom of the family car, drew passengers away from the railways and signalled the virtual end of the rail excursion. Families who previously had merged with other families in a communal display of mass enjoyment now make their own ways to their chosen destinations. Down the motorways they go, dealing with the problems of traffic jams and pile-ups as best they can. And the community singing of the excursionists has given way to the transistorised voices of pop singers, liberally interspersed with the latest information about such things as road repair works, temporary traffic lights and contraflow systems. The railway excursion, like the age of steam which gave it birth, has faded into the realms of nostalgia.

CHAPTER 10

The Hustings.

I am not a political animal. Indeed, there are times when I find the entire business of politics something of a bore. For one thing, I believe we suffer from an excess of it, especially since television invaded our homes, and then there is what I believe to be the artificiality of it all. We have no means of assessing the true ability of the candidate who appears on our screens, for all we see is an image of a person groomed to "come over well" on television. There is no way of penetrating that image and finding what lies beneath.

It was all so very different in earlier years. No candidate could hide behind an image. If he wanted to win the votes, he had to go out into the countryside and earn them, even in areas where he knew his reception would be a hostile one. The hustings were the street corners and the village greens, the market places and the little school halls. There he underwent a searching examination by the voters, to whom heckling was a fine art.

Much of it was light-hearted, as in the case of a man who appeared at a meeting in Wymondham shortly after changing his allegiance from Liberal to Tory. Turncoats were viewed with suspicion in those days and, as he rose to address his audience, he suddenly became aware of the fact that all the men in the front row were wearing their jackets inside out.

Another popular gambit, after the speaker had arrived by pony and cart and disappeared into the local meeting hall, was to remove the pony from the cart, push the shafts through the bars of a farm gate and then replace the horse on the other side. Rectifying the situation in the murky darkness of a Norfolk night was not a happy prospect for the speaker after what had probably been a hectic meeting.

But the tactics were not always as subtle as that. In areas where opposition was solid, candidates often found themselves threatened with physical violence, especially when their listeners had been fortified by drink paid for by the other party. As Election Day grew steadily nearer, enthusiasm sometimes gave way to mob violence, reason was ousted by hooliganism and the local scribes were ever ready to record the details for the next day's newspapers.

It was election fever which, in 1895, brought national notoriety to the townsfolk of Stalham, together with the rather slanderous title of "Stalham Savages". Indeed, it must have been quite a traumatic year in the lives of the people of the district for, in the earlier months, Nature herself had provided a somewhat tempestuous prologue.

On January 25th, during a fearful gale, the old Tower at Eccles was destroyed and much damage was inflicted on the nearby sandhills. Then, on March 24th, a tremendous hurricane — said to have been the severest in England since 1703 — swept across the countryside. So great was the accompanying noise that the service in Stalham church had to be curtailed and, as the members of the congregation were leaving, several of those good folk narrowly escaped injury when the Gable Cross was blown from its position on the porch. Four large barns were demolished and hardly a single house in the parish escaped some degree of damage.

Yet it was left to the townsfolk to provide the night of near-disaster which caused 1895 to be designated "The Year of Wind and Riot". It came in July as the parliamentary election for the East Norfolk constituency entered its final stages. Excitement was rapidly building up to fever pitch and, with just two candidates, party spirit was running high on both sides. Calling for the support of all good Liberals was Mr. Robert Price, the sitting member and, by all accounts, a worthy man to continue in that position. Challenging for the Conservatives, however, was none other than Mr. Henry Rider Haggard of Ditchingham, the author who, following his travels on the African continent, had received acclaim for such books as "King Solomon's Mines" and a long list of others.

On Polling Day, in traditional fashion, the candidates made their way round the constituency in a final effort to whip up the enthusiasm of their supporters. Both men, we are told, were "early astir", leaving North Walsham shortly after eight o'clock in the morning, and some idea of the thoroughness of their efforts can be gauged by the route taken by Mr. Price, as reported in the *Norfolk Daily Standard*. Driving his carriage and pair, it took him to Coltishall, St. Faith's, Horsford, Sprowston, Wroxham, Salhouse, Blofield, Lingwood, Acle, Fleggburgh, Ormesby, Martham,

Ludham, Stalham, Worstead and back to North Walsham. Mr. Haggard, riding in a four-in-hand, did a similar journey, though calling first at Tunstead and pursuing a route which ensured that he and his opponent would not meet on the way. Both men were expected to arrive back in North Walsham at eight o'clock in the evening but, though Mr. Price succeeded in achieving this, the events of the day were to result in Mr. Haggard's return being delayed far beyond that hour.

It was early evening when Mr. Price and his party had arrived in Stalham, and the enthusiastic reception he received bore testimony to his popular support in the town. His horses were immediately unharnessed and the carriage was drawn by an excited throng up to the Railway Station and back to the Swan Hotel. Then, in confident mood, Mr. Price took his leave and set out for North Walsham where, after doing a lap of honour round the town, he retired to the King's Arms Hotel and addressed his supporters from an open window.

At about the time that Mr. Price had been in Stalham, Mr. Rider Haggard and his friends were putting in an appearance at Ludham, and that was where the trouble really started. They met with a hostile reception, during which one of his party, a Miss Hartcup of Bungay, was struck by a stone. The wound was dressed by Dr. Gordon and, undeterred, the cavalcade made tracks for Stalham with two horsemen — Mr. Samuel Kidman of Horning Hall and Mr. Edward Sikes of Ludham — in the lead. At Catfield Mill, a disturbance caused Mr. Sikes to fall from his prancing steed and he, feeling unwell, was left reposing by the roadside.

Their arrival in Stalham was the signal for outright hostilities to begin and, as they reached the Swan Hotel, they were met by an excited mob. It was then that, in the words of a contemporary reporter, "a loafer caught hold of the reins of Mr. Kidman's mare, whereupon that gentleman landed his assailant a crack on the cranium with his whip". This did not please the crowd and an attempt, fortunately unsuccessful, was made to overturn the Conservative carriage. It was now 9 p.m. and Mr. Rider Haggard, in angry mood, retired into the innermost recesses of the Swan.

By 10 o'clock, in the belief that alcohol had played a major part in the disturbances, it was decided to close all the public houses, but at least one of them had already disposed of every drop of beer and spirits on the premises. Still the crowd waited outside the

Swan and, before long, wild rumours began to circulate, one being that the military had been sent for! Then, at 11-30, the measured tramp of men was heard crossing the Railway Bridge and the crowd chilled with horror as a band of one hundred stalwarts lined up in front of the hotel. It then became apparent, however, that they were not soldiers but members of the North Walsham Conservative Club, the leader of whom thus unburdened himself: "We, the members of the N.W.C.C., have come to rescue our friend Rider Haggard from the dastardly treatment he has received at the hands of the inhabitants of Stalham!" He went on to inform the awestruck crowd that Mr. Haggard had won all along the line, a statement which proved to be a classic example of counting chickens before they were hatched for, the following day, Mr. Price was declared to be the winner by 410 votes.

Anyway, protected by his newly-arrived supporters, Henry Rider Haggard emerged from the portals of the Swan and, in a towering rage, declared that Kaffirs, Zulus and Hottentots were nature's gentlemen compared with THE STALHAM SAVAGES. Shortly afterwards, the outraged candidate and his party vanished in the darkness and the Stalham Savages retired to their beds.

News of the night's events spread rapidly and, two days later, a reporter from one of the leading national daily newspapers arrived in the Town to inspect the "smoking bloodstained ruins of Stalham". However, in the words of the contemporary report, "being unable to discover so much as a broken window or an ensanguined nose, he packed his trap and, like the Arabs, silently stole away".

Election Day in 1895 had certainly been a day to remember amongst the local populace and yet, even when it was all over and Mr. Price had been declared the winner, further excitement lay ahead. Still to come was the day of reckoning, when a steady stream of miscreants found it necessary to present themselves before the magistrates at Smallburgh Workhouse and answer for their actions at Ludham and Stalham. There was to be a string of convictions for almost every form of physical violence, as well as such other offences as being drunk and disorderly and using obscene language. But the greatest excitement stemmed from the fact that two men, both well-known though from extreme ends of the social scale, were to be charged with having committed an assault in North Walsham Market Place. As the *Norfolk Daily Standard* stated in its report of the proceedings:

"Seldom, and in all probability never, have the few inhabitants of the immediate vicinity of Smallburgh Workhouse witnessed such an unwonted scene as that presented on Tuesday, when it was generally known that Lord Wodehouse, the heir to the Earldom of the Kimberley estates, was summoned to appear for having committed an assault in North Walsham Market Place on the occasion of a political meeting therein, and that a well-known individual was charged with aiding and abetting his lordship in the commission of the said offence". The "well-known individual" was William Saul, better known as 'Tracky' Saul, a cattle drover from North Walsham, who, in modern parlance, was employed at the time as his lordship's "minder". The victim of the assault was John Gaymer, a highly-respected businessman of the Town and partner in the building firm of Cornish and Gaymer.

Proceedings were due to commence at noon but, long before that time, a large number of people had assembled outside the Workhouse, clamouring for admission. Lord Wodehouse made an impressive entrance, driving up in an open carriage and pair a full hour before the appointed time. Mr. Gaymer arrived more modestly, his pony and trap being driven by his groom, the splendidly-named Goliath Amiss. Even Mr. Price, the successful candidate in the election, put in an appearance, smilingly shaking hands with many of his political friends and opponents. Some idea of the significance of the occasion in official circles can be gained by the fact that the proceedings were under the personal supervision of the Chief Constable of Norfolk, Mr. Paynton Pigott, who had at his disposal a body of some fifty constables drawn from various parts of the county. Fortunately, their services were not required, for the assembled crowd consisted mostly of those who were either defendants or witnesses in the various cases and, in the words of the *Daily Standard,* "they behaved in exemplary fashion".

In the case involving Lord Wodehouse, a seemingly endless procession of witnesses testified as to the happenings in North Walsham Market Place on July 17th. It appears that Mr. Gaymer was standing on a chair addressing an assembled crowd of listeners when Lord Wodehouse, with 'Tracky' Saul at his side, came on the scene and proceeded to make defamatory — indeed blasphemous — remarks concerning the speaker's character. An altercation ensued, during the course of which Lord Wodehouse called upon Mr. Gaymer to come down from the chair. "Come down, you miserable hound", he cried, "and I'll fight you for £50".

THE ELECTION.

POLLING IN EAST NORFOLK.

DISGRACEFUL PROCEEDINGS AT STALHAM.

A LADY INJURED.

The polling took place in East Norfolk yesterday, and was conducted, for the most part, in a quiet and orderly fashion. Unfortunately at Stalham some very disgraceful proceedings took place, to which reference is made further on. The weather on the whole was fine. The early morning was cloudy, and gave promise of much rain. A twelve hours' downpour under ordinary circumstances would have been regarded by all farmers with unmixed satisfaction; but the knowledge that the fields day would keep many of the labourers on the and out of the polling booths probably compensated them for any disappointment they may have felt when the promise of the early hours was dissipated by the brilliant sunshine that prevailed during the greater part of the day. In the afternoon there were a few heavy showers, but these were of short duration, and not sufficient to make work on the land impossible. It seems highly probable this morning will not that the poll when it is declared it is general ly prove to a large one, and a small poll, the Unionist candidate. It admitted, is favourable to to Liberals to know that in will give some confidence the poll was very heavy. This some districts at least Walsham, where 748 voted out was the case at North There is a consensus of opinion of 884 on the register. will be a very small one, and there is a lurking fear in the hearts of some of the Liberals that their candidate, popular as he is in the division.
... vere Mr. R. J. Price (L) and Mr. ... not be at the head of the poll.
... Mr. Pri... ...feated Sir Edward Price 4743, by a majority ... recorded

EAST NORFOLK ELECTION ROWS.

LORD WODEHOUSE AND "TRACKY" CONVICTED.—

THE OUTRAGES AT LUDHAM AND STALHAM.

Seldom, and in all probability never, have the few inhabitants of the immediate vicinity of Smallburgh Workhouse witnessed such an unwonted scene as that presented on Tuesday, when it was generally known that Lord Wodehouse, the heir to the Earldom of the Kimberley estates, was summoned to appear for having committed an assault in North Walsham Market-place on the occasion of a political meeting therein, and that a well-known individual was charged with aiding and abetting his lordship in the commission of the said offence. There were a number of other offences alleged against a lot of individuals for being plicated in the disgraceful proceedings ich occurred at Stalham and Ludham, where the age of Mr Rider Haggard, the Unionist candidate for East Norfolk, was stoned; and the people assembled from the surrounding villages showed r presence the interest which was felt in the se. This chiefly centred round Lord se, who, it may be stated, drove up to the se in an open carriage and pair, at about or at any rate a full hour before the proceedings were fixed to commence. e the Guardians of the Smallburgh nsacting the b... they

Mr. Gaymer declined the offer and tried to continue his address to the crowd, whose excitement had, by then, reached fever pitch. A scuffle ensued, and the voice of 'Tracky' Saul was heard saying, "Now go in, my lord", followed by "I am here, my lord; I will look after you". This he repeated several times for maximum effect. Poor Mr. Gaymer was now in the centre of the milling mob and it was not long before he found himself removed from the chair on which he had been standing.

The big question which faced the Court was, "Did he fall or was he pushed?" Evidence from the many witnesses varied dramatically in accordance with the demands of their political masters, but Mr. Gaymer had no doubts on the matter.

"I was pulled off the chair," he said. "I did not fall. The defendant seized me by the coat and pulled me down. Indeed, but for falling on the shoulders of another man in the crowd I must surely have been injured".

107

North Walsham Market Place, where Lord Wodehouse and 'Tracky' Saul disrupted
John Gaymer's Election meeting.

Lord Wodehouse, it seems, was unrepentant. He admitted that
he had "to a certain extent" lost his temper, but he merely wanted
to ask the complainant a question. He agreed that, if he had gone
into a public hall where a duly constituted meeting was being held
and had dragged the chairman from the platform, it would have
been a far more serious case, but this had been a meeting held in
the public square, where everybody was entitled to go.
Furthermore, there was no evidence that Mr. Gaymer was
chairman — except that he was standing on a chair! Anyway, said
his lordship, "some allowance must be made for political heat and
political excitement".

The magistrates eventually retired to consider the evidence put
before them and, after twenty minutes, returned with their
verdicts. Lord Wodehouse was found guilty of common assualt,
for which he was required to pay a fine of £3.7s.6d and £1.12s.6d
in costs. 'Tracky' Saul, for his sins, was fined £1 plus costs of
£1.12s.6d and immediately enquired as to what term of
imprisonment he would undergo if he refused to pay.

"Fourteen days," said the Chairman.

"Right," said Saul. "I'm not paying. I'll do the time."

"No, you will not," said Lord Wodehouse. "I will take care of all necessary dues and demands."

That being settled, the two men left the Courthouse, with 'Tracky' loudly declaring that he would rather have done the spell in prison and had the money when he came out. So, for that odd couple, the final curtain had come down on the drama of the 1895 Election.

For poor John Gaymer, however, there was still one more scene to be played out, for he had been the victim of another assault a few days before the North Walsham incident, and this was to be the subject of the next case for the magistrates to consider.

The accused this time was John Neal of Paston, summoned for assaulting Mr. Gaymer at Edingthorpe on July 13th. As before, there was conflicting evidence from both sides of the political divide. Mr. Gaymer said the accused continually interrupted him as he addressed the meeting at Edingthorpe Green, but he knew that he would meet with opposition and he paid no attention, even when Neal threatened to "give him something so that he would not be able to get out on Friday (polling day)." It was after the meeting had ended, however, and he was standing on the grass verge by the roadside, that Neal deliberately drove his pony and cart straight at him three times, shouting "Get out of the way — my pony don't like b***** Tories." As a result, he suffered injuries to his knuckles.

The accused claimed that it was an accident, but Mr. Gaymer's groom, the redoubtable Goliath Amiss, avowed that this was not so — the roadway at that point was thirty feet wide and no horseman with any semblance of ability would have found it necessary to mount the verge. Then came Edward Cooke, butler to Lord Wodehouse (that man again!), who claimed that the accused shouted to Mr. Gaymer to get out of the way but, instead of doing so, he "walked into the pony".

The case was to end on a lighter note when, after consulting in private, the magistrates decided that an assault had been committed, though not a very serious one, and defendant would be fined five shillings with fifteen shillings costs. A peal of laughter rang round the Court as the defendant replied, "Lord Wodehouse is going to pay."

As I was saying — elections were a little bit more exciting in the old days.

CHAPTER 11

The Fun of the Fair.

One of the earliest memories of my North Walsham boyhood is of lying in bed on a summer's evening and hearing, through an open window, the sound of distant fairground music. The fair always assembled on the meadow opposite the railway station, and sleep was very reluctant to overtake me as I listened to the strains of the mechanical organs. I visualised the scene, with the hissing of the steam engines and the flickering gas jets, which the older boys were still enjoying, and I wished I was old enough to be there. Then sleep would come and I would dream of joining the showmen and exploring the world in a horse-drawn caravan.

I was just about old enough to ride on the children's roundabout, a hand-cranked affair set up in a quieter corner of the fairground. But even this modest form of entertainment, peacefully pursuing its circular motion, could be surrounded by scenes of frightening ferocity. We Britishers have long been admired by foreigners for our self-control and, above all, for our ever-ready willingness to form ourselves into orderly queues. The trouble is that it was physically impossible to queue for a ride on a roundabout, for there was no beginning and no end. The entire contraption was surrounded by parents — admiring parents whose children were already riding, and suffering ones who were hoping to get their offspring on the roundabout for the next excursion. They were suffering because their objective was not merely to get their children on board but to commandeer the particular motor car, bus, railway engine or aeroplane which had taken their child's fancy. And, of course, it was never possible to predict where the roundabout would come to a halt.

It was when the ride stopped that the trouble started and our national reputation for civilised behaviour was cast aside. Father, with young Freddy in his arms, would wade in towards the fire engine as though he was heading "once more unto the breach" at Agincourt; Mother, as if in training for the January Sales, would drag little Elsie in a headlong dash for the bicycle with pedals which really did turn round. Even then, success was not assured

Children's Corner at Tombland Fair, 1910,

for, only too often, some precocious boy, already in command of the fire engine and its steering wheel and bell, would opt for a repeat ride. Three more children could climb on board, but they could do no more than sit and admire the skill of the driver-cum-bellringer. But round and round they went in a whirl of dreamy ecstacy until, as the showman brought the ride to a halt, they were dragged away with a degree of reluctance which could only be assuaged by a toffee-apple or a paper windmill.

As I grew older, I was freed from parental restriction and, under the care of my older brother, I was able to enjoy the delights of the fair to the full — and what a wonderful experience it was. The crowds were dense and the noise was almost overpowering. Laughter and enjoyment engulfed us. We visited seedy sideshows. We threw darts at playing cards and tossed rubber rings in the general direction of tawdry, but enticing, prizes. We climbed to the top of the Mat and slid frantically down again. We jerked ourselves along the Cake Walk and shunted everybody all over the place on the Bumper Cars. But, all the time, we kept a constant check on our closely-hoarded pocket money lest it should run out before the evening was over.

There are not so many fairs travelling around the countryside these days, and those which remain are very different from those we knew in boyhood. They are brightly-lit affairs, and the quaint melodies of the steam organs have given way to the stridently transistorised music of this modern age. Yet none of the fairs of the past century can compare with those of earlier times when it comes to matters of debauchery, cruelty and general unsavouriness.

Most of the traditional fairs can trace their origins back to the twelfth and thirteenth centuries, when the local Lord of the Manor was granted a charter to hold such an event for the express purpose of raising money. He needed funds to pay his dues to the King and also for the upkeep of the roads and buildings of his Manor. What better way of raising cash than by holding a fair? Sales could be registered and taxed, stalls and booths could be charged for — there was no end to the possibilities.

One place which reaped the benefit of such a charter was Diss where, for nearly 700 years, the annual Cock Street Fair brought fame — indeed, notoriety — to the otherwise quiet market town. Every year, between October 27th and November 1st, Cock Street Green (more recently known as Denmark Green or Fair Green) became the scene of one of the liveliest and most colourful events in the life of the town. Local shops would be closed, with shopkeepers transferring their wares to stalls on the Green, which was fenced off so that everybody could be charged for admission. Farmers and weavers took wool, hemp and cloth for sale to travelling merchants. Much drink was consumed for, not only did the inns do great business, but householders on the Green displayed oak branches from their upper windows to indicate that ale could be purchased within during the Fair. And there was such a vast array of stalls selling every conceivable kind of foodstuff that a writer of the time was moved to express his apprehension concerning "serious disorders in the thousands of stomachs which might become receptacles of the many compounds prepared for the delectation of the public palate". There were gingerbread and toffee stalls, roast chestnut stands, "herrings cooked and herrings raw", hot sausages, dumplings with treacle — and rock in abundance. The assorted fragrances, intermingling with the emanations from the numerous drinking booths, caused the same writer to declare that "the combined odours of tobacco, beer, hot sausages and bloaters are anything but pleasant to one's olfactory organs".

Entertainment was mostly of a simple nature. There were boxing booths and Punch and Judy shows. There were jugglers and tumblers and pretty dancing girls with tambourines. But there were also "attractions" of a less pleasant nature. It was an age when the vicious pastimes of bull-baiting, bear-baiting and cockfighting were not only popular sports but legal forms of entertainment. A contemporary writer has left a graphic account of the manner in which animals and fowls, trained to kill, were encouraged to tear each other to pieces in specially built pits, with large crowds assembled to watch and vast sums of money depending upon the outcome. I cannot bring myself to quote from his description but will merely offer the words of a local rhymester:

Here in the jovial days of yore
The mad bull welter'd in his gore,
The gamesters trembled at his roar,
    In the old days of Diss.

A cock, a bull, a surly bear,
A cur toss'd yelping in the air —
These were the frolics of the fair
    In the old days of Diss.

It seems little wonder that the Victorians would have none of it. In 1872, the Justices of the Diss Division submitted to the Home Office a petition that it would be "for the convenience and advantage of the public that the fair should be abolished". The Home Secretary duly ordered its abolition as from April 16th 1872.

Fair Green still survives as one of my favourite little corners of Diss — indeed, one of the pleasantest corners of Norfolk — and, every now and again, the showmen arrive with their wagons. Then, for a few brief days, the air is filled with the sounds and scents of the fairground, just as it has been for something like seven centuries.

The annual Fair at Ingham was a two-day event, starting on Trinity Monday and sharing the first day with the traditional cattle sale, at which local farmers took the opportunity to dispose of what remained of the season's fatstock. As with Diss, it had ancient origins, for history records that the mediaeval friars held a fair in the village on Trinity Monday to raise money to ransom knights held captive in the Holy Land. However, it was the eighteenth century which saw the introduction of the fat cattle show, a tradition which lasted until the 1960s.

But it was the funfair which was the attraction for most of the local populace. The travelling showmen would arrive on the Sunday and begin the process of setting up their attractions on a field near the village inn. Then, as the two-day wonderland gradually took shape, excitement spread through the surrounding area, with villagers for miles around wondering what fresh innovations would be on offer and what new tunes would be issuing forth from the fairground organs. There were times when it almost seemed that Trinity Monday would never come.

Yet the arrival of the Fair was not universally welcomed by the people of Stalham and district. Indeed, there were many who were appalled by the drunkenness and fighting which sometimes accompanied it and who condemned the affair as "The Devil's Spree". Then, in order to remove themselves and their children from the temptation, they organised a counter-attraction in the form of an outing to Eccles Beach. There, while the parents sat among the sand dunes munching their cheese sandwiches, the children played games and ran races on the beach, safely removed from the depravity of the fairground! Transport to Eccles was provided by means of four or five farm wagons, all towed by a single steam engine. It was not the fastest of journeys, for the engine was restricted to a speed of four miles per hour through Stalham and five miles per hour on the open road. But they were in no hurry and, as the illustration shows, they were even prepared to stop on the way and, climbing out of the wagons, were happy to have the event recorded by a photographer.

During the glory days of the village fair in Norfolk there were a number of fairground families who travelled around the county providing fun and excitement for the local populace. There were the Grays and the Gizzis (I well remember the colourful display on Mrs. Gizzi's rock stall), and there were the Smiths and the Thurstons. There were such men as Alf Stocks, George Summers and Jim Crighton. But from all those generations of showmen there is one man who is probably remembered with the greatest degree of affection — 'Rhubarb' Underwood.

There were, in fact, three men who qualified for the name of Rhubarb, for it became a hereditary title, though only through two generations. The founder of the Underwood dynasty and, indeed,

114

The Trinity Outing leaving Stalham.

A roadside stop on the way to Eccles.

Showmen and their ladies, Woolpit Fair, 1897. Left to right: Alf Stocks, George Summers, – Abbot, – Osborn, B. Poll and Jim Crighton.

Showmen exercising their horses, early 1900s.

the man who first earned the nickname was John Rock Underwood. He was born some time between 1860 and 1870 and, in his early years, was employed by a showman named Dack. It was a time when fairground folk did not travel particularly long distances, for motorised traffic was still a thing of the future and they relied solely on natural horse power.

It was Mrs. Dack who unwittingly caused John to acquire the strange nickname. More specifically, it was Mrs. Dack's partiality to rhubarb which brought it about, for she had a passion for the stuff amounting almost to an addiction. "Any time you're out", she would say to John, "and you see any really nice rhubarb, will you bring me some home?" And John frequently obliged. Then came the occasion when Mr. Dack was due to make an early start to travel somewhere on business, and his wife wanted to make sure that he had a hearty breakfast before he set off. Accordingly, the evening before, she gave young John some money and sent him down into the village to buy half a dozen eggs. John duly arrived at the village shop, where the first thing his eyes lighted upon was some absolutely first class rhubarb.

"Ah", he thought, "Mrs. Dack would love some of that − I'll take her some back".

The trouble was that, having bought the rhubarb, poor John had no money for the eggs. History does not record what Mr. Dack eventually had for his breakfast, but his wife had her favourite delicacy — and John acquired the nickname of 'Rhubarb'.

When John later married, he and his wife produced a family of eight offspring, but they never became as widespread as some of the other fairground families, for six of the children were girls, several of whom married men of other callings. Elvina married a showman in the shape of Tommy Smith, but it was mainly left to the two sons to continue the fairground tradition.

The elder of the two was Jack, who differed from many of the travelling showmen in having a home base in Norwich, from which he would travel on some of the shorter trips and to which he would return each night. It was when he was on one such trip that fate dealt a cruel blow for, while setting up his swinging boats on the Green at Martham, he succumbed to a fatal heart attack.

The younger son was Walter, and he is the Rhubarb Underwood who is still remembered with such affection by so many of his former patrons. It would be impossible to list the villages where his memory still lives on; Ludham and Reymerston, Briston and Martham — he covered them all. But it is the nature of the man that is best remembered, for he was a man of utter sincerity and honesty, a man full of love of people — and a man loved by all who knew him.

The fairground folk travelled about so much that most of their offspring were born "on the road", and Walter was no exception. He made his entry into the world at Litcham in 1900, when his father was working Litcham Fair. For most of his life he lived in the elegant caravan which he always referred to as his wagon. He did have a conventional house for a short while when he bought Marsham Foundry with the idea of using it to make fairground equipment and rides. Within two or three years, however, the call of the road became too strong and, when Eastern Counties Farmers made him an offer, he sold out and set off again on his travels.

It cannot be said that Walter rushed headlong into matrimony, for he was 46 when he married his Violet. Equally, he took his time over the plunge into parenthood, for he was 54 when Violet presented him with their one and only child, a son named Perry. Perry was more conventional than most of the fairground folk in that he was born in the Norfolk and Norwich Hospital. Quite a few years later, Perry confided to me that, as a young lad, he viewed with a marked lack of enthusiasm the possibility, when he was older, of being called Rhubarb. He was proud of the family title, but he did not wish to inherit it. When the time came, nobody called him by that nickname, and his father was the last in the line of Rhubarbs.

After the war, Walter regularly spent his winters in Wymondham, and it was there that my friendship with him developed. He would set up his van and all his equipment in a far corner of the King's Head Meadow, that hallowed stretch of green adjoining the public house of the same name, where Billy Goffin was mine host. The two of them had some sort of agreement although, having known both men, I am sure there was nothing formal about it. It was more likely just a question of Walter saying "I'll make it right with you" — and he always did. Then, having got on to the site, he needed electricity for his wagon and for the rides which he sometimes operated at week-ends, and again there were friends to offer help. Indeed, if we wanted to find whether Walter had arrived on the meadow, there was no need to go down there and have a look. Just opposite was an ironmongery business run by the brothers Clive and Denis Clarke. All we had to do was to go round to the back of the shop and, if one of the windows was slightly ajar and a cable was coming out and running down to the meadow, we knew that Walter was in residence. Once again, I feel sure there was no question of metering or working out how much power he used. It was simply a question of "I'll make it right with you" — and Rhubarb always did.

There then came the time when the people of Wymondham decided that they needed a new community hall to serve the town's growing needs. A committee was duly formed, fund-raising began and a site was found. The situation chosen for the new building was part of the King's Head Meadow — including the very corner where Rhubarb spent his winters. I happened to be chairman of that committee and, before long, news reached me that he had grave misgivings concerning the coming of this new hall. He had made up his mind that there would no longer be room for him, and nobody could persuade him to the contrary. I decided to give him my reassurance, and I made my way accross the meadow and tapped on the door of his wagon. Looking back in retrospect, I have often wondered whether, at that moment, he thought I was there to give him notice to quit, for his face bore an unusually

Walter and Violet Underwood.

serious expression. But I gave him my promise that he would never be asked to leave and, immediately, the cry rang out: "Violet, put the kettle on and make a cup of tea for the dentist". It was the first of a multitude of cups of tea which I was to share with them in their wagon.

He persisted in calling me "the dentist" for quite some time until I managed to convince him that I had a name. Then I had similar difficulty in persuading him to use my Christian name rather than the formality of "Mr. Bagshaw" — it was not in his nature to presume upon a friendship.

Over that first cup of tea, Walter became a happy man, but he insisted that he would "make it right" with me. I told him that under no circumstances would the committee accept any payment from him, for his presence was costing us nothing; indeed, it was adding another dimension to the social life of the town.

At the end of that winter, on the day that Walter set off on his travels, I happened to be in Norwich. That evening, I had a call from one of the Clarke brothers to say that Rhubarb had looked for me before leaving but, being unable to find me, had left something for me in their shop. I duly collected what turned out to be a bag full of money, all in pennies, threepenny bits and sixpences. I cannot recall the exact total, but it was an odd amount and had obviously not been counted — it just seemed the right amount to give us. Once again, Rhubarb had "made it right".

Eventually, Walter began to speak of some property which had caught his eye at Wells. He was in his sixties and fairground life was not all glamour to the men who worked it. It was a tough routine, and young Perry was not yet able to play a part in running things. Also, he was concerned about Perry's future. He had given his son a better education than he had ever had, and he wanted to assure him of a degree of security to go with it. Thus it was that, in 1965, he decided to take over the property at Wells. He said his last goodbyes to Wymondham and started a new life at the Pop Inn down on the quayside. Later on, Perry was to take over the adjoining amusement arcade but, in the years that followed, they made not one penny profit out of the café — the only profit came from the amusements. The reason for this is easily explained, for the café became a kind of club where, at any one time, as many as a dozen men would sit mardling and drinking tea for which he never charged them.

But this was Walter's idea of heaven, and he was thoroughly happy until, in 1980, a bit of the sparkle went out of his life when he lost his beloved Violet. But he had two compensations — one was that he had the business, which was a great help, but the main thing was his son. In the years that followed, he and Perry became closer and closer — not just father and son but the closest of companions.

When Walter Underwood died in 1986, at the age of 85, he left a reputation of being a man of honour, integrity, love and compassion. There must be many people whose lives, like mine, were the richer for having known him.

CHAPTER 12

Beachmen of Yarmouth and Gorleston.

A hundred years ago the beaches at Yarmouth and Gorleston were bustling places throughout the summer months. It was the age of family holidays, and the demands of the visitors were modest in the extreme. It was the sea and the sand that brought them to the coast, and they asked for little else; many, indeed, were content to spend each day sitting in a deck chair and making the most of the "change of air".

Nowadays, incoming holidaymakers are waylaid by such a profusion of entertainments along the Front that many of them never get as far as the beach. In those earlier days, however, the situation was reversed. If they wanted to spend their time on the sands, that was where their needs would be catered for, and the beaches became hives of activity. For those who wished to swim there were bathing machines and the horses to pull them down to the water's edge. There were beach huts and rows of little white tents — and deck chairs by the hundred.

There were stalls offering refreshments in great variety. A cup of tea, an ice cream, a plate of cockles — who could ask for anything more? Back in the 1880s, George Martin Holmes was selling fish from a barrow between the Jetty and Britannia Pier. It was a somewhat arduous occupation, for the regulations decreed that he must not pitch his barrow at any one position for more than half an hour at a time. He then graduated to a beach stall, later taken over by his son, who shared his father's Christian names. The younger George offered an array of little plates of cockles and whelks at a halfpenny a time and a hunk of bread at the same price, with vinegar and pepper for his patrons to use according to individual taste. And he would sell you bloaters by the box to send home to your friends. To this day, the family is still selling fish at Great Yarmouth, though no longer on the beach.

When the appeal of the beach began to wane, there was a wealth of entertainment to be enjoyed. The grown-ups could go for a spin along the front in a horse-drawn carriage or they could take a trip out to sea or along the inland waterways. Yarmouth had some fine

George Holmes' shellfish stall on Yarmouth beach.

Bloaters to send home to your friends.

Goat carts waiting for their young passengers.

The Concert Ring.

pleasure ships. There was the *Queen of the Broads,* built in the town in 1889; her sister ship the *Yarmouth,* built six years later; and *Resolute,* a comparative youngster built at Millwall in 1901. And there was a fleet of smaller boats which operated from the beaches and took off as soon as they had a full load.

The youngsters were mostly content to paddle and build sand castles, but there was always a ready audience for the Punch and Judy shows. Then, if they felt like going for a ride, what better mode of transport could there be than a trip in a goat cart? These delightful symbols of a past age were highly popular and, in 1910, there were no fewer than forty of them touting for custom.

Then there were the concert parties, and even they gave their performances on the beach. Most of them took place in what was known as the Concert Ring, a circular arena near the spot where the Marina was later to be built. On the seaward side stood the raised, covered-in stage, illuminated by four gas lamps, one at each corner, and with flags fluttering high above. Around the entire area there was a canvas screen of sufficient height to prevent passers-by from watching the entertainment without paying. The large auditorium was similarly lit by gas but, as it was completely open to the elements, the size of the audience tended to be affected by the weather conditions.

There are still faint memories of Dunn's Concert Party performing there. Mr. Dunn himself, with his thick black beard, sat at a small table at the side of the stage as he introduced his company of entertainers. Wearing a bowler hat and armed with a gavel, he was the epitome of the music hall chairmen of the time. Mr. Dunn junior was the male singer, always introduced by his father as "the robust tenor", and there was a comedian who rendered the comic songs of the day. Most of these have long been forgotten, but there is one that partly lingers in the memory. It concerned a group of people endeavouring, with great difficulty, to rescue a huge creature from the sea. The last refrain is difficult to forget:

> "And when ashore we got her,
> We were glad we hadn't shot her,
> For 'twas fat old Mrs. Potter,
> Poor thing!"

Pride of place amongst the entertainments presented in the Ring must surely go to Chappell's Promenade Concert. It was

Chappell's Promenade Concert.

renowned for its diversity of talent, with singers and dancers, black and white minstrels, orchestras and the ever-popular performing poodles. The crowds flocked there in their hundreds — if the weather was kind. Mr. Chappell's daughter, who looked after the business side of the operation, kept her eyes turned to the heavens and it is said that, every time it rained, she would sit sobbing in the ticket office. The Ring survived from the turn of the century until 1934, when it was swept away to make room for the Marina.

In the thirties there was one corner of Yarmouth beach which we never failed to visit when making our holiday trips to the town. It was the spot where Fred Bultitude produced his amazing sand sculptures, using such basic tools as a wooden knife, a small fork and his hands. As young children, we were always taught to build our future on solid foundations, but Fred was a man who literally carved his career out of sand.

He had been disabled by polio at the age of three and it was in 1927, when he was seventeen years old, that he started his work on the beach. His first creation was a huge representation of a stallion and this became the all-time favourite with onlookers over the next three decades. It was also its creator's personal favourite and he estimates that, in the course of his career, he produced it at least 600 times, which probably gives the clue to the state of perfection he was able to achieve. It also gives an indication of his extreme degree of patience for, not only did some of his scenes take as much as twelve hours to produce, but also there was the certain knowledge that the next high tide would wash the lot away.

In the early years he depicted scenes from the Great War but, as time went by, other subjects, many of them topical, took their place on the beach. Notorious murderers were portrayed, as was the *Girl Pat*, the fishing boat in which a lone man tried to sail across the Atlantic. There were kings and queens in state, a nubile mermaid, and even Popeye with his motorbike. One of Fred's grandest pieces of work was his Loch Ness Monster, carved in protest against the local council which, he claimed, was demanding too high a fee for his licence. The monster was supposed to represent the council and had forty spikes along its length and battery-operated eyes which lit up.

Not only was Fred Bultitude a man of great patience but he was also forever amenable to helpful comment or criticism. His portrayal of *Bluebird,* the car in which Sir Malcolm Campbell broke the land speed record, was seen by Sir Malcolm's son Donald, who pointed out one or two technical faults. He gave Fred a photograph of the car, thus enabling him to correct the offending details.

Just before he retired in 1960, Fred produced The Creator. It was a representation of Christ on the Cross and around it, carved in the sand, was the inscription:

THE CREATOR WHO CREATED ME
TO CREATE SUCH WONDERFUL WORK IN SAND.

With so much activity on the beaches, it is not surprising that there should have been the occasional mishap or, indeed, tragedy. One of the worst of such happenings occurred in the early 1900s when three naval vessels were anchored in Yarmouth Roads, dressed overall with flags and bunting, and boats from the beach were busily engaged in taking trippers out for a closer inspection. One such boat, carrying eight passengers, two musicians and a crew of three, was involved in a collision with a fast-moving steamship and sank in a matter of seconds. Seven passengers were

Gorleston Pier, the scene of William Adams' first rescue.

rescued, but the other six occupants of the boat were drowned, making it one of Yarmouth's worst-ever tragedies.

There were many other incidents which, without prompt action, might well have had disastrous consequences.

On a summer's day in 1875 a little girl was sitting on one of the wooden piles by the edge of Gorleston pier. Suddenly she slipped and, as she sank beneath the surface of the deep water, she let out a piercing, panic-stricken scream. At that moment fortune smiled upon the girl for, further along the beach, there was a young lad who, although only eleven years old, was already a proficient swimmer. Hearing the scream, he ran to the spot and, diving in, brought her back from what would certainly have been a watery grave. The boy was William Adams, and that rescue was the first of what was to become a lifetime of life-saving. Now he lies in his last resting place in Gorleston cemetery in a grave which looks just like the many others around it — except for the stone which stands at its head. It bears a carving of a man diving into the sea to rescue a stricken swimmer and below his name are added the words: "who saved 140 lives from drowning".

William Adams was born in Gorleston in 1864, the son of Abel Adams, a well-known Trinity pilot of that parish. On leaving school, he took up employment as a tinplate worker with the Smith

Dock Trust Company but, like his father, he was much more at home in a maritime setting than in the mundane routine of a shore-based occupation. He therefore acquired alternative employment as a bathing hut attendant and swimming instructor on Gorleston beach. His talent for swimming was legendary and he became known locally as "Gorleston's human fish". He was at one time a member of Norwich Swan Swimming Club, holding that organisation's certificate of proficiency and winning some 60 prizes. He coached some of the best swimmers of the day and gave tuition at many schools and clubs, acquiring in the process the title of "Professor" Adams.

To William Adams, Gorleston beach was the nearest thing to Heaven, and it was there that most of his exploits took place. In 1896 he distinguished himself by rescuing two men at once . They were visitors from Norwich and, when one of them was swept out by the ebb-tide, the other man entered the sea in a rescue attempt and himself got into difficulties. Adams was alerted and swam back to the beach with both men together. The visitors showed their gratitude by presenting him with a fine new bathing hut.

In spite of the fact that he stood a mere 5 feet 6 inches, he was endowed with great physical strength, a fact which led the local newspaper to describe him as "a fine specimen of English manhood and English pluck — the greatest acquisition of this popular bathing resort".

His strength proved useful on another occasion, when he swam back to the beach with a rowing boat in which were four extremely distressed youngsters who had been swept out to sea by the tide. Then there was the day when he dashed along the entire length of the pier and dived fully-clothed into the sea to rescue a schoolboy.

His very keen sense of hearing also stood him in good stead, notably when he saved a lad from drowning near the ferry. It was a dark evening and, as he walked home with some of his workmates, he faintly heard cries for help from among the fishing boats. With not so much as a word, he dashed away and dived to the rescue.

His exploits brought him much recognition during his lifetime. He received numerous Royal Humane Society vellums, seven gold and silver medals together with others in bronze, and an assortment of illuminated addresses. The Carnegie Hero Fund presented him with a cheque, and from grateful members of the public he received a gold watch and chain, a marble clock and various ornaments.

William Adams, Gorleston's 'human fish'.

William Adams died in 1913 at the tragically early age of 49. When the end came, it was as the result of an action which typified the life of the man. All that year he had been far from well, suffering from a liver complaint brought on, it was said, by too much exposure to salt water. Confined to his home at 199 Bells Road, he pined for the beach. The summer season was pursuing its course and he yearned to get down there amongst his beach huts and tents. Then, one day in August, he felt slightly better and he pleaded with the doctor to be allowed out of the house. The doctor relented, but with the strict proviso that he was not to go down to the Front and certainly not even to think of going in the sea.

Adams, of course, headed straight for the beach. There he was happy for a while until there suddenly came a cry for help from somebody in difficulty in the sea. It was impossible for him to ignore it. He went into the water and, helped by others, rescued the struggling man. But then he became the one who needed help. They had to take him home and put him to bed, and there he stayed. That final rescue was in August 1913; he died in the October.

They hailed him as a hero, for the memory of his exploits was still fresh in their minds. The *Yarmouth Mercury* carried a glowing tribute. "In all his rescues", the paper said, "he always put aside any thought of personal risk, acting on the moment with one thought uppermost — that the life of a fellow creature was in peril. Such characteristics make the true hero".

But the *Mercury* credited him with having saved 87 lives, whereas the friends who erected his memorial stone gave the figure as 140. We shall never know the true figure, but it matters not one bit. William Adams was a man whom the town can remember with pride — a hero fit to stand beside that other great Gorleston rescuer, lifeboat coxswain William Fleming.

CHAPTER 13

Wymondham —
Friday Sale and Whit Thursday Sports.

One great advantage of living in the country was the ease with which you could dispose of unwanted furniture and other such items — you simply sent everything to the weekly sale. There they all were — the rickety tables and threadbare sofas; old pictures that might be worth a fortune and other old pictures that definitely weren't; garden tools and bikes, carpets and beds — you could get rid of almost anything at the saleground.

Every town of any size had its weekly sale and, as each one had its own particular day, it was possible to visit a different one each day of the week if one felt so inclined. Wymondham's Sale was on Fridays, as it had been for as long as anybody could remember. It had come into being centuries ago as a stock sale for farmers but, in more recent times, the livestock had gone elsewhere and the Friday Sale concerned itself with more mundane matters. There was butter and garden produce, old lawnmowers and the many items which masqueraded under the splendidly comprehensive title of bric-a-brac.

It was as long ago as the year 1203 that King John granted the town the right to hold three annual stock fairs, and these continued until well into the nineteenth century. Records of those fairs give a good indication of the vast numbers of sheep which were raised in the area around the town, but the presence of those animals in the fields brought problems, for there were felons abroad in the countryside. Cattle and sheep rustling was an ever-present problem, in spite of the fact that the penalty for such an offence was either transportation or, in extreme cases, death.

One wonders whether Wymondham was unique in having this problem, for one of the old pieces of country doggerel still remembered by older residents went:

"Wymondham Sheep-stealers, Wicklewood Owls,
Hackford Duzzies and Hingham Fules".

Certainly the problem was great enough for the local farmers

Fairland Street, Wymondham, showing the entrance to the saleground.

to band together and form the "Wymondham Association for Prosecuting House-breakers, Horse-stealers, etc., etc.", and rewards were regularly offered in an effort to apprehend the villains.

By the late nineteenth century Wymondham had become renowned for its magnificent agricultural shows and on three occasions between 1881 and 1895 the County Show was held in the town. Then, in 1905, the Wymondham Agricultural Society came into being to promote the interests of "Wymondham District Farmers". At the head of the energetic committee was William S. Hall, a local farmer who specialised in the breeding of pedigree white pigs. He was also a Justice of the Peace and was held in high regard throughout the county.

It was William Hall who, around 1910, took over the saleground, the site on which the regular Friday Sales took place. Before long, he joined forces with Harold Palmer, thus bringing into being the firm of W. S. Hall & Palmer which, for something like three quarters of a century, was to become a highly-regarded feature of the county's agricultural scene.

Then, as the twentieth century progressed and brought with it greater mobility for both men and animals, so livestock became a steadily diminishing feature of the weekly sales. Cattle and the like still found their place at the Wymondham Sale until after the Second World War, but now they are all gone, leaving only memories — memories of cattle and sheep being driven along Fairland Street every Friday; of the tap of sticks and the clatter of boots as farmers and drovers made their way through the town; and, perhaps most splendid of all, the memory of the prize bull which a proud Albert Cross paraded in the Market Place, such a fine beast that it had to be taken to the weighbridge at the railway station to discover that it tipped the scales at $27\frac{1}{2}$ hundredweights.

Now, the farmers may have stopped coming, but the world and his wife are there, poking and prodding, sifting through boxes of old books and speaking in hushed whispers lest their bidding intentions should become known. Then the bell rings and the auctioneer emerges from his office, looking rather like a bishop in a mission hut — much too grand a man to bother himself with selling cabbage plants at fifty pence a box.

Of course, one of the great dangers of the Friday Sale was that one could easily be overcome by the excitement of the occasion and find oneself buying objects for which one had no conceivable use. One man who occasionally succumbed to the temptation of impulse buying was Billy Butcher, and he should have known better, for he was a regular. Billy had a smallholding a few miles out of town and every Friday he would harness up his pony and cart, load up with trays of his vegetables, and drive in for the Sale. Leaving his wife Hannah to look after things, he had three objectives in mind: hopefully to sell, possibly to buy and, most certainly of all, to meet up with his cronies. When it came to the question of buying, he was on safe ground with such things as day-old-chicks or bags of fertiliser, but it was a different matter when something out of the ordinary caught his eye. There was, for instance, the umbrella. It was a very smart-looking umbrella, just the sort of thing Hannah would be glad of. He made up his mind to buy it — if the price was right. Luck was on his side and it was knocked down to him for a shilling.

He was a happy man as his pony took him back to Wreningham. He could hardly wait to see his wife's pleasure at the gift he had brought back for her. But Hannah, more pennywise than Billy, was a bit dubious.

"I hope yew han't bin wearstin' yar money", she said.

"No, that I han't", said Billy. "Thass a bargain. Only cost me a bob".

Then Hannah did what Billy should have done before he bought the umbrella. She opened it up, to reveal a veritable pepperpot of holes in the fabric.

"Just yew look at that", said Hannah. "Yew silly ole fule — you've wearsted yar money".

"That I han't", said Billy. "That'll dew fer muckin' about indoors".

My last visit to the Friday Sale was by way of saying goodbye. They were closing it down to make room for a Health Centre and I wanted to have one last look before they moved to a new site and the old one became just a memory. As it happened, that final look around became something of a nostalgia trip, for somebody must have been clearing out some ancient cottage and there, arrayed on a table, was a selection of household objects. They class them nowadays as bric-a-brac — "collectors' pieces" — but in my early boyhood they were the very essentials of everyday life.

My eyes immediately fell upon the centre piece of the display. It was a tall, graceful oil lamp with its slim brass column polished to perfection and its bowl and shade of fluted ruby-coloured glass glinting in the sunshine. I would have liked to buy it, but I remembered all the cleaning and wick-trimming that my parents and my grandmother had done, and the washing and polishing of those fragile glass chimneys.

I turned my gaze to the two ancient flat irons, pitted and scratched by many a fire. I suppose somebody would buy them, though I had no wish to acquire them. I remembered our last one, pensioned off when we "went over to the electric", serving out its time as a doorstop. My mother had three irons, which she heated in a wire contraption hanging on the grate. As one cooled down she would change it for another, and I can still hear the sizzling sound as she delicately tested its temperature with spit. She had beside her a piece of brown paper with some candle tallow on it, and she would rub the iron on this to make it run smoothly. Then, now and again, there would come her plaintive "tut, tut" as a stray soot mark showed itself on her clean white linen.

I ignored the flat irons and transferred my attention to the objects which stood around the paraffin lamp. They were three splendid chamber pots, one bearing a floral decoration in the most delicate shade of pink, one similarly adorned in blue and the other being plain white. Two young ladies were inspecting one of them. "Just the thing for pot plants", said one. "I was thinking of it more as a container for Class 4 at the Flower Show", said the other. I smiled inwardly, for they were both too young to remember the chamber pot in its heyday. Tucked unobtrusively beneath the valance of the bedstead, it was an essential convenience on a dark night when the nearest source of relief was a windswept walk away at the bottom of the garden.

The good folk of Norfolk have never been slow to celebrate a special occasion, and the people of Wymondham in particular have long had the reputation of throwing themselves wholeheartedly into any such festivity. When Queen Victoria reached her Golden Jubilee on June 21st 1887, the entire day was given over to a celebration befitting the occasion, beginning with a morning service in the Abbey Church, attended by some 1500 people. Then, in a remarkable segregation of the sexes, the working men sat down at noon to a meal of roast beef and plum pudding, while at 4 p.m. their wives and children partook of a hearty tea. As soon as they had finished, everybody made for the King's Head Meadow, where a crowd of 4000 people gathered to watch a programme of athletic sports.

Ten years later, for the good Queen's Diamond Jubilee, a cricket match was followed by a communal tea and, once again, a sports meeting. Then, to celebrate the Coronation of Edward VII in 1902, the main feature of the day was, yet again, a programme of "Old English Sports".

The main reason for the popularity of sports meetings in the town was the existence of Wymondham Athletic Club, which had amongst its membership a number of very fine athletes. For a long time, Whit Thursday had been a recognised holiday in the town, as it was, I believe, in many parts of the county, and that was the day when the Club traditionally held its Annual Sports. Then, in 1884, the committee decided to make an all-out effort to spread the Club's fame by attracting competitors and spectators from further afield. An attractive prize list was the first essential and, accordingly, a London wholesaler was invited to come and display his wares in the Assembly Room at the King's Head. A fine array of awards was selected, and the ploy worked. At that first open meeting competitors came from as far afield as London and Lincolnshire — indeed, the runners almost outnumbered the spectators. Among them was C. G. Wood, acknowledged as the "Amateur Athletic Champion of England, France and the

The scene on the King's Head Meadow at the Whit Thursday Sports.

Continent". He was suitably impressed, declaring that in all his travels in England and France he had seen nowhere with more promise of successful meetings than in Wymondham.

The next thing was to attract more spectators. The following year an approach was made to the Great Eastern Railway Company suggesting they might offer reduced fares for people wishing to travel to Wymondham for the Sports. The Company agreed and, for the 1885 meeting, cheap excursions ran from stations all over Norfolk, with two special trains from Norwich. People flocked to Wymondham and soon the town was almost bursting at the seams, with the public houses enjoying a phenomenal surge in business.

The scene on the King's Head Meadow was such as had never been seen before and was, indeed, a sight which we are never likely to see again. A large grandstand was erected on the far side of the arena and, further along, there was a grand marquee in which the President entertained favoured members of the gentry. On the King's Head side a row of wagonettes was drawn up, offering a splendid view of the proceedings, and the rest of the perimeter was packed with a vast crowd of spectators. There was a selection of tents – one for the judges, another into which the athletes retired to change into their running gear, and others

Jesse Harvey, the Wymondham Bellman.

which offered refreshments to the crowd. And there was much to entertain onlookers apart from the athletic events. Throughout the day a sword-swinger demonstrated his skills in various parts of the arena whilst, in intervals between races, the boys of Watts' Naval Training School demonstrated their prowess in such things as physical exercises and gunnery. And all the while, keeping the public informed as to what was happening, there came the voice of Jesse Harvey, Wymondham's Town Crier, resplendent in his magnificent costume.

But it was the Sports that drew the crowds, and they were on offer in a diversity of forms. There was flat racing over a variety of distances, and there were hurdle events in which the hurdles were the real thing — the wooden agricultural type which, unlike today's pop-up variety, presented a physical barrier to the competitors. A runner who failed to give one of them sufficient clearance inevitably took a tumble and, quite apart from having no further interest in the race, could quite easily find himself nursing a painful ankle injury.

Then there were the cycle races, and it was probably those events which created the greatest excitement, particularly after a period of rain. There was a prepared track with banking on the corners, but everything took place on the hallowed turf of the King's Head Meadow, and this frequently offered problems when wet. Like their riders, the machines came in a variety of forms, from penny farthings to others which more befitted the talents of their owners. Contemporary photographs portray the two types of machine ready for the start of a race, but it is difficult to imagine them taking part in the same event. A little bit of posing, no doubt.

The effect of weather conditions on the cycle racing was well reported in the *Norwich Mercury* after the Sports of 1908. "During the afternoon", said the paper, "there were several incidents, the most serious of all occurring in the three-miles scratch bicycle race open. When taking one of the corners, Allen fell and brought Skeel, Summers and Robertson to the ground, the last mentioned being hurled among the spectators. Skeel and Summers remounted but it was found that Robertson was very badly shaken. Rowell was also unfortunate in falling when about 60 yards from the winning post and was badly bruised".

A Norfolk favourite who unfailingly attracted the crowds was Dave Cutmore, the first man ever to cycle up Norwich's Gas Hill and still regarded by many as one of the finest racing cyclists East

Cycle races attracted a wide range of machines.

A hurdle race in progress.

140

Anglia has ever produced. He was a frequent trophy winner, both at Wymondham and elsewhere, but even he occasionally came to grief. Cyril Wigby, a native of Wicklewood now living in retirement at Bungay, recalls that his parents were regular visitors to the Sports, where they sat on chairs by the trackside to watch the racing. Before the 1907 meeting there had been overnight rain which had made the grassy surface slippery and, coming round the last bend at speed, Dave parted company with his machine, flew through the air, and landed on Mrs. Wigby's lap. Neither of them was hurt, but Cyril's mother was so upset that she never went to another Sports meeting. However, as Cyril points out, his mother lived to the age of 86 and Dave Cutmore reached 75, so it seems that their brief encounter did them no lasting harm.

One local lad who tasted success at the Whit Thursday Sports was Willie Gordon Smith, better known in later years as Billy Smith, the proprietor of Wymondham Swimming Pool in the period betwen the two World Wars. He was born a few miles from Wymondham at Morley St. Botolph, where his parents carried on a grocery business. By the time he reached his teens he had become a proficient cyclist, having started with a boneshaker and graduated by way of a penny farthing to a "real" bicycle with pneumatic tyres. When he was sixteen his parents took over the village Post Office, and the delivery of the mail became Billy's responsibility. He was supposed to carry out this task on foot but, as his round extended to almost six miles through Morley and the adjacent parishes of Deopham and Hackford, he found it more to his liking to use his cycle.

He then discovered that there was a special cycle race at the Sports for competitors who lived within six miles of Wymondham. It was a one-mile race, five laps to the mile, and he decided to enter. From then on, he spent all his spare time practising, taking the opportunity also to inform as many people as possible that he was riding in the Wymondham Sports. Then, as the big day drew nearer, he found himself being assailed by an increasing feeling of nervousness, which reached its peak as he arrived at the King's Head Meadow.

"I went into the dressing room", he said, "and put on my shorts, and I shall never forget old Mr. Harvey ringing his bell and shouting 'Competitors for the One Mile Closed Race, come out!' There were crowds of people standing close to the ropes and all I could see was faces, but they all looked alike to me".

There were about five others in the race and, as they were handicapped according to age, three of them got a few yards start on Billy, and they went off at a terrific speed. It was not until the third lap that he managed to pass one of them and, as he did so, he heard some of the spectators shouting "Go on, Billy". Then, as he steadily gained on the others, shouts were coming from all round the track: "Go on, Billy. Keep it up". As they entered the last lap, he could see that he had a chance and, urged on by the spectators, he took over the lead with just half a lap to go.

"I didn't see any more of my competitors", he said, "until I had finished the race and, as I returned to the dressing room, I couldn't believe I had won first prize".

But then he heard the bell ringing out and Jesse Harvey shouting, "Winner of the last race — W. G. Smith". He went up to receive his prize and was immediately surrounded by friends, all wanting to have a look. It was a splendid set of fish, fowl and meat carvers.

The Whit Thursday Sports continued, year by year, for a quarter of a century, bringing fame to the town and creating a tradition which seemingly would last for ever. In 1904 there was an innovation in the form of horse jumping events, and there was a presentation of a silver salver to S. R. Huson, "probably the oldest athlete in England", who had competed in Wymondham for twenty successive years. The Sports of 1908 were as successful as any that had preceded them but then, for reasons which history does not record, it all came to an end. Perhaps the organisers wanted to hand over the reins to others but were unable to find volunteers. Whatever the reason, the tradition of 25 years was no more. The townsfolk were sad as they mourned the loss of their historic event.

On Whit Thursday in 1909 there was no influx of visitors from the rest of the county. The people went about their business in their normal daily way, and the King's Head Meadow stood deserted. 'Old Chowes' Blazey, a well-known local character, reflected the sense of mourning which was abroad in the town as he made his way through the quiet streets. Dressed in a black frock coat and silk hat, he carried a placard bearing the inscription:

WYMONDHAM IS DEAD

SPORTS SUICIDE

CHAPTER 14

North Walsham —
The Family Business.

For centuries Norfolk's market towns have played a vital role in the social and business life of the county. Neatly spaced out as they were, each one was the focal point for its own area, supplying the needs of the folk who lived in the scattered villages which surrounded it. Lacking present-day mobility, the journey into town was accomplished on foot or by bicycle, with the more fortunate ones travelling by horse-drawn transport. Once there, however, everything they could possibly want was readily available.

North Walsham was typical of such towns, offering a far greater diversity of shops and business premises than exists today. Many were huddled around the ancient market place which, history tells us, was originally the Lord of the Manor's Home Farm, complete with its own windmill. Then, with the arrival of the Flemish weavers and the prosperity they brought with them, it was found to be more profitable to rent out the land for market stalls, which eventually became permanent buildings. The mediaeval stall was seven feet long and, though I have not investigated the matter, I am told that the frontage of many of today's shops can be measured in multiples of seven feet.

The great thing about the shops of my boyhood is that they were nearly all completely local — they were family businesses, owned and operated by people who lived among us. There were a few exceptions. The International Stores and the Star Supply Company faced each other across the market place. There was the British and Argentine Meat Company and also Brenner's Bazaar (later Peacock's and eventually Woolworth's), but most of them, large and small, were run by people we knew. One feature was the vast array of little shops, so numerous that one wonders how they all managed to make a living. Ladies like Connie Peacock, Lily Bruce and Martha Harvey supplied the town's smoking needs; Jimmy Craske and George Howlett purveyed a wide selection of fish; John Hall and Harry Carpenter offered fruit and vegetables. Billy Mount and Albert Kimm would repair your boots, while

Mr. Grey and his 'shop that sold everything'.

Frank Chittock would cut a piece of leather to size so that you could do it yourself. The list was endless, but one will live forever in blessed memory — Mr. Grey's "shop that sold everything". Kelly's Directory listed his business as "Hardware and furniture dealers, tobacconists &c." It was that final &c that told the full story, for there were very few items which could not be obtained from Mr. Grey. From doormats to paraffin lamps, chamber pots to dinner services and every other conceivable household requisite — they were all there. There was Lifebuoy soap for bath night, Sunlight for washday, and Monkey Brand for scrubbing the kitchen table, not forgetting Robin starch and bluebags. There was flour and paraffin, vinegar and sugar, tobacco and tea, both Brooke Bond and the local favourite, Lambert's B. O. P.

If one wondered how that little shop on the corner of Bacton Road and Back Street could hold it all, the sight of his delivery cart was even more amazing. Every day Mr. Lawrence from Felmingham took the vehicle out, laden to overflowing, on his trips around the surrounding area. His main cargo was paraffin, with everything else stacked precariously above and around the tank. Items of food tended to acquire an added flavour because of the proximity of the oil, but nobody seemed to bother. Mr. Lawrence was just one of a legion of paraffin men who daily made their journeys around the country roads of Norfolk in the service of local housewives.

It would be impossible to write of Mr. Grey's shop without mention of his Annual Sale. It was not really a yearly event — he had one whenever he had a selection of goods which would otherwise be left on his hands. One of the regular attractions was wallpaper, which was reduced from something like threepence to a penny per roll. A constant succession of children, despatched by their respective mothers, would arrive with instructions to pick a pretty pattern in pink or blue or whatever colour Mother fancied. It was always a single roll, for it was not destined to adorn a wall — it was new lining paper for the shelves in the pantry.

Arthur Griffin was another man who could supply almost everything, though in a different field. Arthur spent his working life in an Aladdin's Cave of bicycles and spare parts and, when he died in 1991, he could justifiably lay claim to have been the longest-serving shopkeeper in North Walsham. He had started his business in 1924 when he was fourteen years old, and he always vowed that he would never retire — and he never did.

Arthur Griffin in his Aladdin's Cave of bicycle parts.

He first set up business in his parents' house in Vicarage Street, his working capital being the ten pounds he had managed to save during his schooldays. Four years later he moved to Market Street, on the corner of Mitre Tavern Yard, and it was there that he steadily accumulated an awe-inspiring collection of the bits and pieces he needed for carrying out repairs. The walls and the floor were festooned with wheels and frames, mudguards and every other part of a bicycle, in such a state of disarray that no Mrs. Mopp could possibly have attempted to clean the place. Yet Arthur knew where everything was, and it was a very rare occasion when he was unable to supply a cyclist's needs.

There were only two things about Arthur's shop which changed with the passage of the years. One was the lighting system, for in 1928 the establishment was lit by gas mantles, which survived until he "went over to the electric". The other was the bikes he sold. In earlier times they were British-made roadsters which have long since become collectors' items. More recently they were mostly foreign — and Arthur got no pleasure from selling them. He was bemoaning the demise of the British cycle industry when I paid my last visit to him for a chat, not many weeks before he died.

"Look at that lot", he said. "Foreign rubbish. There in't the quality in 'em nowadays 'cause hardly any of 'em are made in this country any more".

But Arthur was that rare creature, a thoroughly happy man. He came smiling through the depression of the thirties and then the years of war which followed. And he remained a confirmed bachelor — I suppose it could be said that he was married to his bikes.

My outstanding memory of Arthur Griffin is of the day when he sold me my first carbide lamp. I was nine years old and he, already five years a businessman, was nineteen. He offered me a demonstration of the lighting procedure and I watched enthralled as he brought forth a flickering flame which, at the time, seemed an absolute flood of illumination. Later developments such as the dry battery and the dynamo were to reveal the inadequacy of the carbide lamp, but it did at least enable the after-dark cyclist to obey the dictates of the Law, even though it was sometimes guilty of behaving in a somewhat temperamental manner.

But to the schoolboy cyclist of that time the carbide lamp was much more than simply a source of light — it was a status symbol. Its presence on the front of his machine indicated that he had at last been granted parental permission to ride his bike after dark — one of the major milestones on the road to adulthood. Yet, sadly, it was a carbide lamp which brought about my earliest brush with the Law — and it wasn't even my lamp! Furthermore, by a strange quirk of fate, the incident occurred just outside Arthur's shop.

I remember that it was a Tuesday, for that was always Cub Night and we had all gathered in the wooden hut by the railway embankment just off Aylsham Road. Then, when Gladys Smith, our cubmistress, closed the meeting, seven or eight of us retired to the back of the hut for the ritual lighting of our carbide lamps. It was dark, but all went well — except for Duggie Brown. Whether he got the mix wrong or what else could have caused the disaster I know not, but his lamp caught fire and the flames shot high in the air. There was then nothing to be done except to extinguish it and wait for it to cool down before having another go. But we didn't all want to hang about, so we told Duggie to get on his bike and we would take him home in convoy. Down Aylsham Road we went like a posse of cowboys with Duggie in the middle in case the town constable was on the prowl. He was a marvellous copper and we all respected him, largely because he knew each and every one of us and, more significantly, he knew our parents.

We turned into Market Street and everything was going according to plan until, suddenly, out of the shadows at the entrance to Mitre Tavern Yard strode the familiar figure of the constable. Up went his hand.

"Right, boys — dew yew stop! Now, Duggie Brown, your lamp in't alight".

"In't it?" said Duggie. "Well, that was a little while ago". He was telling the truth. It had been alight — well alight.

"Well", said the policeman, "if that was alight a little while ago I can soon find out, can't I?"

At that point he started to peel off his woollen mittens. Of course, we knew what he was about to do, but we daren't say anything. He put his hands forward and clasped them around Duggie's lamp. Needless to say, it was still almost red hot, and the effect was dramatic in the extreme. He shot several feet in the air and went into a torrent of swearing which seemed to last for about ten minutes, never using the same word twice. We later reckoned that those few minutes just about completed our education. But we never heard anything more about it — I think he was in a hurry to get home and rub some butter on to his blistered hands.

George Fuller (in uniform, left of centre) poses with colleagues in front of the St. John Ambulance, 1924.

Of course, that sort of thing could never happen nowadays. I sometimes think a lot of the fun went out of cycling when we gave up using the carbide lamp.

So many of the shops of the thirties have now left the scene. The drapers' stores of George Fuller and Frank Loads, together with the Marjoram Brothers' gents' outfitters, have gone, never to be replaced.

Fuller's was established in 1844 by a Mr. Bullimore, whose daughter married George Fuller. On the death of the founder, George gave it his own name and also made it the headquarters of the St. John Ambulance Brigade, of which he was not only divisional superintendent and secretary but also the ambulance driver. He was not simply a draper — in the terminology of the day he described himself as a hosier, milliner and ladies' outfitter. His advertising slogan, proudly proclaimed on his carrier bags, was: "More choice, more value in fashion, coats, underwear, corsetry, curtains and dress fabrics" — hardly the snappy epithet of today, but certainly more descriptive.

I have to admit to a lack of personal knowledge of the interior of

Fred Randell and his original shop. *(See page 152)*

The enlarged shop, built in 1897.

George Fuller's shop. It was one of the few local establishments where my mother never took me, for most of the stands were liberally adorned with ladies' underwear — hardly a suitable sight for the eyes of an impressionable youngster! I have been told by a lady informant, however, that the shop specialised in "the really reinforced corsets, the kind where the wearer had to get somebody to put their foot in the middle of their back to get the strings tightened up".

Frank Loads' shop was another which was out of bounds to me, for its contents were of a similar nature to those which George Fuller displayed. As young lads, however, the shop had a great fascination for us, for legend had it that Frank habitually gave each of his customers a cigarette. This meant, of course, that he must have a fair supply of cigarette cards and there were frequent occasions when the most daring among our number, having first ensured that there were no lady customers within, would open the door and enquire, "Got any cards, Mr. Loads?"

Situated as it is in a farming area, it is not surprising that some of the town's businesses should have come into being to supply the

151

needs of agriculture. The milling firm of Barclay, Pallett & Co was a sizeable concern with depots at Aylsham, Cromer, Wroxham, Gunton and Cawston, together with staithes at Bacton Wood and Wayford Bridge. In the earlier years of this century their little fleet of wherries — the *Ella, Ethne, Elizabeth* and *Bertha* — plied the waterways in that part of the county. Also engaged in the milling business was the firm of Cubitt and Walker, with their headquarters at Ebridge Mills and their depot at the M. & G. N. railway station in the town.

The name which became best known to the farming community, however, was probably that of Fred Randell. Randell's was founded in 1820 with an ironmongery shop in the Market Place and a foundry in Northrepps, which was moved to Bacton Road in the town in 1865. The shop originally stocked such conventional items as crockery and lamps, baths, pails and garden tools. Before long, however, Randell's were producing a wide variety of agricultural implements, for which the pig iron was brought up the North Walsham-Dilham Canal to Swafield Wharf and then carted to Bacton Road. Business thrived and, in 1897, the shop was rebuilt on a much grander scale as the name of Randell became a household word in the world of farming.

Yet there were three local names which were destined to achieve much more widespread recognition in very different areas of business. William Alexander Le Grice led a double life as an outfitter in the Market Place and a purveyor of groceries and provisions in Church Street. His son, however, was not attracted to the life of a shopkeeper. Having inherited a love of flowers from his mother, Edward Burton Le Grice opened a nursery in 1920 and proceeded to devote his life to the cultivation of roses. During the years that followed, he became one of the country's acknowledged experts in rose hybridisation, producing seventy-five new varieties and winning an impressive array of awards in the process. He received the Queen Mary Memorial Medal for British Rose Hybridists and was elected to the National Rose Council, with a place on their panel for judging new roses. In 1965 he was prevailed upon to write his book "Rose Growing Complete", which was immediately recognised as the most complete book on the rose yet published.

To watch Edward Le Grice at work in his glasshouses was to witness an artist in action. He was a tender, gentle man and every action in the cross-pollination process bore witness to the love of

Edward Le Grice at work in one of his propagating houses.

roses which had been with him since early boyhood. He acknowledged the support he received from the two women in his life, and his book was dedicated:

"To my Mother
who taught me to love roses
and to my Wife
for whom I grow them."

He was a man of vast experience in the world of the rose. "As a child of twelve", he wrote, "trying to grow my first rose trees I learned by bitter failure that enthusiasm is no substitute for experience. As a callow youth I learned from the knowledge of those who had grown rose-wise by generations of practice. In maturity I would share with others the delights of a lifetime spent in rose growing".

I was fortunate enough not only to watch him at work but also to benefit from his ever-ready advice. My garden has never been without roses. Now, as I revel in such delights as the deep red, damask scented *Ellen Mary,* the brilliant, unfading yellow of *Allgold* and the ever-changing gold and crimson shades of the fragrant *My Choice,* I remember with gratitude the man who gave them birth.

From horticulture to building. When the dictates of the Elementary Education Act of 1870 made it necessary for the town to have a purpose-built school, the man chosen for the task of building it was Robinson Cornish from Knapton. The product of his work, built to accommodate some 600 children, still stands at Marshgate, together with some more modern additions.

Within a year or two Mr. Cornish joined forces with John Gaymer, setting up business at Millfield and forming a building company which, almost immediately, was to receive nationwide recognition. For Cornish and Gaymer were no ordinary builders — they were also stonemasons and ecclesiastical carvers. They had amongst their company some of the finest craftsmen in the land, notably Charles Henry Simpson, whose first piece of work, executed when he was sixteen years old, was the carving on the altar of the Parish Church.

There is much evidence of their work in the town, but it can also be found much further afield and in far grander surroundings. The Cathedrals in Norwich and Durham are the settings for some of it, as also are Winchester College Chapel and a host of churches.

But there was one family whose fame spread even further. In 1880 there had come to the town a craftsman who, with his successors, was destined to achieve a high degree of acknowledgment, not only for his family name but also for the town itself. That man was Robert Farman, whose family had, for several generations, been engaged in the country crafts of basketmaking and thatching in the area around Horstead and Coltishall. His decision to move to North Walsham brought with it one great problem, for he needed a copious supply of water with which to soak the willows used in his work and, at that time, there was no piped supply in the town. It was for that reason that he chose as a site for his business Garden House in Aylsham Road, for it was in close proximity to the communal pump which served that area of the town. There he began building a reputation for the quality of his craftmanship and he remained in business until, in 1919, his son returned from war service to take over the reins.

That son was Robert William Farman, known to most people as Billy. By then the waterworks had been built and, being no longer dependent on the old pump, Billy moved further along Aylsham Road. There he entered upon the golden era of thatching, using

The young princesses' house that Bob Farman re-thatched. *(see page 156)*

only the best Norfolk reeds from reserves and reedbeds all over Broadland. In due course he was joined by his son who, though christened William Robert, was known as Bob, and who, I am happy to say, was a contemporary and schoolmate of mine. Bob retains vivid memories of the reeds being carried across the roadless marshes to the waiting wherries, particularly the *Lord Roberts*, sailed by Jack Gedge from Swafield and, in its day, probably more famous even than *Albion* is today. Unloading took place either at Wayford Bridge or Barclay & Pallett's quay at Wroxham and then the journey was completed by road.

The reputation surrounding the name of Farman continued to spread and, in 1939, the family firm received its highest accolade in the form of a Royal Command. The people of Wales had made a gift to the then Princess Elizabeth of a kind of miniature house, which was to be erected in the grounds of Windsor Lodge. It was originally roofed with straw thatch but, following a fire, a replacement with Norfolk reeds was decided upon. Farman's were selected for the task and it was Bob who travelled down to carry out the work. The operation took about a fortnight to complete, after which Bob's father received the Royal Warrant. This must have been a great source of pride to all concerned and it seems rather sad that, when Billy Farman died, the Warrant died with him.

Bob then transferred the business to Cherry Tree Lane, from where the Farman reputation was destined to spread even beyond the confines of Britain. In the mid-fifties he received a request to thatch the roof of a house in America. It was in Maine and for no less a person than Pamela Woolworth, a member of the renowned chainstore family. Bob recalls the 15 railway wagons full of reeds which, together with the men who were to carry out the task, were loaded into the cargo boat for their transatlantic journey. The work took about two months to complete and was followed by other orders in the U.S.A., including a house on Long Island, New York.

Sadly, time never stands still, and Bob has now retired. Furthermore, he was the last of his line to bear the proud title of "Farman, Thatcher, North Walsham". After an unbroken record extending to 108 years, the wagons no longer trundle in and out of the town carrying their loads of best Norfolk reeds. But a thatched roof often has a greater permanence than mere mortals and, long after many of us have gone, there will be a host of examples still proclaiming the loving care and skill which went into their construction.

CHAPTER 15

What's in a Name?

There can be little doubt that anybody who comes into the world with the surname Clarke will, at some time in his life, be dubbed 'Nobby'. Similarly, the Millers, the Whites and the Browns are quite likely to acquire the nicknames of 'Dusty', 'Chalky' and 'Buster'. There seems to be a singular lack of imagination in present-day nicknames when compared with those devised by our antecedents. Indeed, some of those earlier creations were so bizarre that one is left wondering how they were acquired.

Even the derivation of the word 'nickname' is itself open to question. Professors of Linguistics, those worthy folk who study the origins of words, tell us that it is derived from the 15th-century word eke, meaning additional. Thus, an additional name became an eke name which, by corruption, became 'a nickname'. This sounds perfectly logical and is probably correct, but I have a preference for the less erudite explanation in which I have always believed. This, again mediaeval in origin, stemmed from the people's fear of the Devil, whom they knew as 'Old Nick'. They believed that he was everywhere, watching everything that took place and listening to every word that was spoken. Hence, when they wanted to talk about somebody, they invented for that person a new name which was known amongst themselves but unknown to the Devil. It was a name to fool Old Nick — a nickname. A trifle romantic, perhaps, but it gets my vote.

My belief in this explanation is reinforced by the fact that it arose from superstition, and there is nowhere in this county that one will find a greater plethora of nicknames than amongst the North Norfolk fishermen — and their lives have been dominated by superstition for centuries.

The *Louisa Heartwell*, the last of the pull-and-sail lifeboats to operate from Cromer, was a fine old craft, and her record of service bears testimony to the courage and skill of the men who sailed in her. It is many years since she left the scene, swept aside by the arrival of engine power, but she still occupies a special place in the hearts of those who knew her. Yet, quite apart from her

The *Louisa Heartwell* and her boatload of nicknames. The young Henry Blogg is second from the left in the back row.

well-chronicled exploits, there was something else about her which made her unique, for she carried among her crew what must surely have been the widest range of nicknames ever assembled together.

There were 'Bentley' Kirby and 'Young Dinger' Blogg. There were 'Buckram' and 'Butler' Balls and the cunningly-named 'Mus' Cox and 'Crow' Rook. The Harrison family was represented by 'Measles', 'Ponsey', 'Kally', 'Jimmy Buttons' and 'Billy Buttons'. There were 'Kite' and 'Will Doll' Rix, 'Loady' and 'Baby Sam' Nockels, not forgetting 'Sailor' and 'Young Sailor' Allen. Finally, the Davies family supplied 'Captain', 'Lantern' and 'Old Joe'.

But there was one youthful member of the crew who never acquired a nickname in the true sense of the word. He was known to his colleagues simply as 'Ry' and was, of course, Henry Blogg. Young Henry, brought up and trained in the ways of the sea by his stepfather, John James Davies, had first donned the cork lifebelt and the woolly pirate-type hat in 1894. He was just eighteen and, though it was to be some time before he was to earn the acclaim which lay ahead, he was already exhibiting some of the characteristics which marked him out from the rest. To begin with, unlike his colleagues whose faces were adorned with luxuriant beards and moustaches, he went through life clean-shaven. For most of the time he paid regular visits to the local barber though, on one occasion, he bought himself a safety razor so that he could do the job himself. Unfortunately, he took the word 'Safety' too literally, with disastrous results. It was then that he reverted to his lifelong belief that a professional task should be left to the professionals.

The other thing that set him apart was that he was both a non-smoker and a non-drinker. He had tried them both, but liked neither. When he smoked his first cigarette, he was asked what it felt like. "Stupid", he replied. "Like an ole pig with a bit o' straw in its mouth". He never tried a second one. His first contact with alcohol came about by the force of circumstances and his wish to conform. In those days, part of the lifeboatmen's income came from cash awards resulting from rescues and, in particular, the salvaging of vessels which otherwise would have been lost. The money went to the coxswain who would periodically call the men together at a local hostelry for the share-out. It was inevitable that, on these occasions, part of the money went to the publican in payment for the drink consumed while the men were there. It was on Henry's first share-out that he encountered alcohol for the first time. History does not record how much he consumed but, later that night, his stepfather and brothers heard the unsteady sound of his arrival back at the cottage, followed by his noisy climb up the narrow staircase to his bedroom. Once there, he called down to them, "Thass alright. I aren't drunk". But, of course, he was and he felt even worse in the morning. It was then that he vowed never again to touch alcohol, and he never did.

Strangely enough, it was Henry Blogg's teetotalism which at one time threatened to bar his progress to the position in the boat which later brought him such wide acclaim. It was at a time when the coxswain of the *Louisa Heartwell*, 'Jimmy Buttons' Harrison, was temporarily disabled from carrying out his duties. A substitute was needed until he regained full fitness, and Henry's name was put forward. Unfortunately, there were many crew members who feared that a teetotal coxswain might bring to an end the tradition of festive apportionments in various public houses around the town, and the name of George Rook was also proposed. When it was put to the vote, the question of skill triumphed over drinking habits — but only just, for Henry Blogg won by a single vote!

That was in January 1909. Later in the year, Jimmy Harrison's health was such that he found it necessary to resign as coxswain and, on December 4th, sixty fishermen, together with committee members, met at the Red Lion Hotel to appoint his successor. This time there was no need for a vote, for Henry Blogg was elected unanimously. Thus, December 4th 1909 signalled the birth of the most magnificent era in Cromer lifeboat history.

Unlike Sheringham, where nicknames tended to become hereditary titles, those in Cromer never seem to have been handed down. I can only think of one man who inherited his father's nickname, and that was Edward Allen. His father, Walter, was always known as 'Catty' Allen, and Edward became 'Young Catty' — but only until he left school. By then he had acquired a slow and deliberate way of speaking and somebody remarked that he talked like the Prime Minister. Hence, he became 'Boy Primo' or simply 'Primo'.

Allen was a dominant name in Cromer at that time. There was James Allen ('Sailor') and his brother John ('Wessun'). There were also 'Bussey', 'Buck', 'Chippy' and others. But it was 'Primo' who became one of Cromer's great lifeboat heroes. He served for nearly forty years in the boats, and that great record only came to an end when he tragically became the first man to lose his life in the service of the Cromer lifeboats. It was on October 26th 1941, a Sunday, when the *English Trader* went aground on Hammond Knoll in the most atrocious weather conditions. The story of that rescue is nothing less than an epic, and it should be essential reading for anybody with Norfolk blood in their veins. Conditions were so bad that nobody other than Henry Blogg would have attempted what seemed an impossible task. By the time the *H. F. Bailey* reached the stricken vessel, five of the 49-strong crew had been washed overboard and drowned. Then, when still a hundred yards away, the lifeboat was hit by a tremendous wall of water which capsized her, tossing five of her crew into the water like corks. They were Henry Blogg, aged 65 and a non-swimmer, second coxswain Jack Davies, Henry Davies, 'Sid' Harrison and 'Primo' Allen.

By what Henry Blogg later described as "the Hand of Providence", the *H. F. Bailey* miraculously righted herself and the five stricken crew members, all near death, were eventually hauled aboard. The lifeboat reluctantly made for Yarmouth, where four of them recovered from their ordeal. For 'Boy Primo', however, it was too late. He died from exposure and exhaustion. The following day the *H. F. Bailey*, with a replacement crew member for their lost colleague, went out again to the *English Trader* and, in somewhat improved conditions, successfully brought ashore the 44 survivors. It was a story which, if written as fiction, would have been dismissed as being too far-fetched to be believable.

There can be no doubt that, in Sheringham, nicknames were a necessity of everyday life. The town remained little more than a compact fishing community long after Cromer had taken the plunge into holiday resort status, and many Shannocks left the area to seek a livelihood elsewhere, their descendants still to be found all along the coast from the Thames Estuary to Grimsby. For the remainder, with only a handful of family surnames, and the added complication of handing down Christian names through successive generations, identity became something of a problem. It is said that, in the earlier years of this century, there were no fewer than sixteen men named John Henry Grice living in Beeston Road alone. Even as recently as ten or fifteen years ago, it was useless to go to Sheringham and ask for Bob West or Henry West, for there were five of the former and four of the latter. But ask for 'Teapot' or 'Downtide' or 'Joyful' and there is no problem.

'Squinter' West.

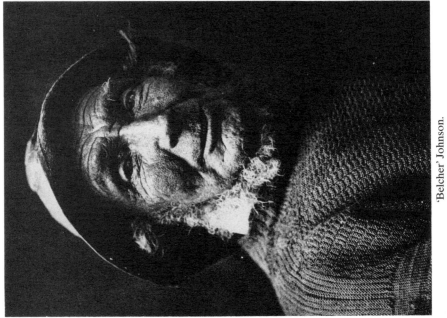

'Belcher' Johnson.

'Old Pegg'.

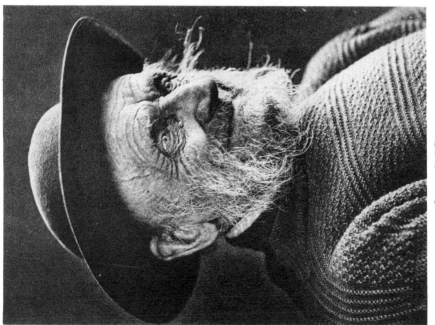

'Latter-day' Cox.

163

Thus it was that nicknames came to be handed out with something approaching wild abandon. The origin of many has been lost in the mists of time, but there are some that give more than a hint as regards their holders' physical attributes or personal behaviour. The Craskes included 'Sausage', 'Squeezer', 'Cock Robin' and, because of their style of walking, 'Bounce'. The Grice family boasted 'Chicken', 'Cheese', 'Butter Balls' and 'King Kong'. The Johnsons seem to have been rather badly treated with 'Spider', 'Frog', 'Maggot', 'Snouts' and 'Belcher'. Men with some sort of Naval connection were given the statutory title of 'Tar' and among the Bishops there were 'Billy Tar', 'Jack Tar', 'George Tar' and 'Bob Tar'. Even the womenfolk sometimes became involved, as in the case of Martha Hannah Bishop, the wife of 'John Tar', who was known as 'Marthanatar'.

One nickname for which I regret being unable to discover an explanation is that of 'Latter-day' Cox. The dictionary definition of latter-day is "modern" but, as one looks upon the benign features of that dear old man, one can only regard that as being singularly inappropriate in his case.

Among the Wests there were 'Teapot', 'Red-Eye', 'Squinter' and 'Never-Sweat', but there were others which, having been passed through several generations, are still borne with as much pride as if they were knighthoods. Robert Henry West, coxswain of the lifeboat until a few years ago, delights in the title of 'Joyful', first bestowed many years ago upon his grandfather, who was known for his joyful singing of gospel hymns as he sailed his boat.

Then there was the Henry West who, as a young lad, mistook his father's instructions to turn the boat uptide and did the reverse manoeuvre, thus earning the name 'Downtide'. It became a greatly revered title which passed to his son, Henry E. West, then to his grandson, David West, and now has doubtless reached his great-grandson, another Henry.

Yes, indeed. When it comes to nicknames, Sheringham tops the lot.

CHAPTER 16

Simple Folk.

People nowadays, we are told, are tending to live longer than did our forefathers in the earlier years of the century. I have no doubt that statistics are available to prove this fact, and yet I harbour memories of folk who, in the past, lived to "a tidy old age". Indeed, centenarians were by no means uncommon.

A friend of mine had a grandmother who came near to reaching her hundredth year and, had it not been for her irrepressible skittishness, she might well have done so. When she was well into her nineties, she could walk four miles without stopping or taking a rest and, ludicrous as it may seem, she had a habit of trotting down the stairs and jumping the last three to the hall floor. Unfortunately, when she was 96, she did it once too often and died as the result of a broken thigh, though still in possession of all her faculties.

A Norfolk centenarian well known to my friend was Will Gibbs, a boatbuilder in Stalham. He was endowed with great strength and seemingly limitless energy and, in the words of my informant, "a rare big ole feller he wor". Indeed, my friend recalled the day when he encountered Will, then in his mid-nineties, striding along the turnpike with a garden spade slung over his shoulder. Though Will's energy was something of a legend in those parts, my friend was unable to resist enquiring as to where he was heading with the spade.

"Tha'ss on account o' my poor boy Jim", said Will. "He ha' got the rheumatics that bad he can't stoop to dig his garden, so I'm a-goin' to turn over a bit for him".

Will's "poor boy Jim" was then 72, but the exertion obviously did the old man no harm, for he lived well into his 103rd year.

Another local centenarian was Mrs. Cubitt of the Manor Farm at Sea Palling. Her final age is not known to me, but she was still hale and hearty when she entered her 107th year. Right up to the age of 100 she insisted on getting up every day at five o'clock in the morning, and on her 103rd birthday her friends arranged for her to have a celebratory trip in one of the new-fangled motor cars which were appearing on the county's roads. Her reactions to the experience were slightly mixed.

"I reckon tha'ss reg'lar fulery flyin' along in that manner", she said. "But, Lord love me, that fare really nice, that that dew".

But one of the most remarkable of the county's earlier centenarians must surely have been Hannah Ives of Happisburgh, whose grave can be found in the parish churchyard. She lived alone in her little cottage, preferring — as she put it — "ter dew fer meself", and there she supported herself by doing any little jobs that came her way. She was something of a living wonder and, when she reached her hundredth birthday, she was still able to read her Bible and to thread the finest of needles without the aid of spectacles.

It was something she achieved on her 73rd birthday, however, which marked her out as somebody special, for she decided to celebrate by going to visit her son John. The fact that he lived twenty miles away in Yarmouth and that her only way of getting there was by walking did not deter her. She set off from Happisburgh at five o'clock in the morning and made just one stop on the way — "to drink a glass o' porter at a little afore one". Then, off she went to complete the journey.

"I had my dinner along wi' John and rested altogether tew hours", she said. "Then, at three, back I come, a-swinging along wi' a great picklin' cabbage tied up in a red handkerchief hanging over my shoulder. And then, bor, that was turned eleven when I got hoom and, if you'll believe me, I was that tired I fared as if I could hardly get me butes off afore I was asleep".

So Hannah Ives led her self-sufficient life until she was nearly 102 when, being cruel to be kind, they took her away to the workhouse. She lasted there until she was 103 and then, in the words of one who knew her, "the poor old lady died o' nuffin on'y a-grizzlin' to think she'd been put away".

There was nothing really unique about Barney Baker. There were many men like him, liberally sprinkled throughout the Norfolk countryside — men with bewhiskered, weather-beaten faces and a fund of knowledge which had come from life rather than books; men who would utter the least possible number of words if they didn't "take to" a person, but who would recite endlessly to anybody who found favour in their sight. And, above all, men with faces as expressionless as a block of wood while they related some almost unbelievable story from the past, only to suddenly flash that twinkle in the eyes which made it impossible for the listener to know whether it was truth or just a gigantic leg-pull.

But when it came to matters concerning the land Barney was always serious, and he was a much better weather forecaster than the men who came on the wireless and talked about warm fronts in the Azores and winds in the Heligoland Bight. He knew, because he studied Nature. "You can't improve on Nearture", he used to say. "Jest you tearke a leaf out o' Nearture's book and you oon't go far wrong". And he spoke with an authority born out of a lifetime's study of the natural world. He always knew what kind of winter lay ahead and from which quarter the prevailing wind would blow. He knew, because he watched the little shrews going about their business. They always made their holes away from the direction of the prevailing winds and, if a hard winter was in prospect, they dug a bit deeper. They seemed to have advance information denied to mere humans, and they passed it on to old Barney.

Barney was a horseman and, in spite of the long hours he spent each day working on the land, he still found both the time and the enthusiasm to cultivate the kitchen garden at the back of his cottage. Furthermore, not only were his vegetables renowned as the finest in the district, but they also involved little in the way of financial outlay, for everything he needed was readily available around him.

In the first place, he always saved his own seed. Then, of course, the many horses and cattle which were part of his daily life provided him with all he needed in the way of manure. Finally, there was the question of pesticides, and Barney had, for instance, a particularly effective way of dealing with slugs. Though he had no access to the many lethal pest-killers now in use, still he managed to keep his tender vegetables free from attack by predators — and again on a cost-free basis. During the course of their married life, he and his wife had accumulated quite a collection of teacups which had become parted from their handles. Nothing was ever thrown away and these cups, pressed down to soil level at strategic points in the garden, were brought into use as traps. Then came the question of bait and, for this, he had ready access to ample supplies of left-over beer from the Cross Keys, where he was a regular, and much-valued, patron. Every evening Barney would go on his rounds, pouring beer into the cups, and then, as darkness fell, the slugs would emerge and, in their unsuspecting eagerness, would fall victim to the lethal brew. This was organic gardening at its best and there was not even any need to remove the dead slugs the following morning — the hedgehogs did it for him. They lived under the hedge at the back of Barney's toolshed and they had established their own kind of bridle path through the garden, calling at each teacup on the way. First they would eat the marinated slugs and then they would drink the beer before staggering off on their nocturnal wanderings. The hedgehogs gave Barney's cuisine a four-star rating, and every morning the cups would be licked dry. When the cold weather arrived and there were no more slugs, they retired to their resting place behind Barney's shed, no doubt dreaming all winter of the summer delights to come.

The prospect of retirement had little appeal for Barney. He had worked for fifty years for the same master and had earned a rest, but there were those two horses which had shared his working days. He was the only man who had worked them and, like him, they were getting on in years. His soul was in torment, but his boss came up with the answer. On the day that Barney retired, so also were his two horses put out to grass. Barney couldn't quite see their meadow from his window, but they were near enough for him to stroll up there each day, pockets bulging with apples and sugar lumps.

I have never ceased to marvel at the unique bond which so often developed between a teamsman and his horses. It was a two-way relationship and, just as Barney's heart beat a little bit faster as he drew near their retirement meadow, so they, at the first sign of his approach, charged joyfully to meet him like the two-year-olds they had once been. Somehow, I cannot imagine Barney falling in love with a tractor.

The same could well be said of Charlie Smith, who was a country blacksmith before he went into local politics and sat on the Labour benches of Norwich City Council. His change of status led to his becoming better known as C. L. Smith rather than by his friendly Christian name, but the change was purely cosmetic — his heart remained that of the countryman he had always been. He was a simple versifier whose only piece of writing known to me was "The Team-man's Lament", published in a local journal in 1947. I suppose it cannot be called great poetry, but it was written from the heart and, indeed, in the language which was Charlie's native tongue. I believe it to be worthy of repetition:

I arnt agin tractors. Not at all.
They du git over some ground.
No doubt we want more on 'em.
But I du miss my hosses.

You carn't call a tractor good company.
Will that hear ye come inter the yard
An' let ye know tha's pleased to see ye?
That ha' got lugs med o' steel
But du they tahn backards to listen
Ter ivery wahd you say to 'em?
No fear they don't, not them.

That earnt no good sayin' 'Woosh'
Nor yit 'Cubbear' to a tractor.
That hearnt got a nice sorft nose
Like welvet
What snubble up agin yer pocket
Fer a napple or a bit o' sweet.

Why, a hoss is werry near a Christian.
That know Sunday from week-day.
Go you inter the yard a Sunday mornin',
You'll find 'em all layin' down.
They know werry well thass Sunday.

D'you remember them two brown 'uns?
Prince and Captain we naamed 'em.
I was there when they were born,
Exactly a twelvemonth atwin 'em.
I browt 'em up, I brook 'em in
By the side o' thar old mother.

Ah, they wor *a pair o' hosses,*
The best round here for miles,
Lovely ringles all over thar coats,
Dapples our old man useter call 'em.
Thar coats were like a bit o' silk.

You carn't curry-comb a tractor
Nor yit you carn't coox it.
If you du that'll bahn yer hand
Or else freeze it.

Ah, tractors are all werry well.
They wholly git over some ground.
No doubt we want more on 'em,
But still thass a masterpiece
How much I miss my hosses.

Barney Baker's record of fifty years with the same master was certainly a splendid achievement, but even that seems almost mundane when compared with the Pettingale brothers of Castle Rising. All five of them spent their lives working on the Castle Rising Estate and, when the last one finally retired, their combined length of service had reached the staggering total of 300 years. The first one to cease work was Richard, and he could hardly be said to have plunged headlong into retirement. He was 79 when he left the land and, when asked why he had left it so late, he replied simply: "I han't ever thought about it afore now".

On the great day, the five brothers put on their best Sunday suits and strolled down to the Black Horse Hotel. There, fortunately for us, somebody had a camera to record the occasion as the quintet posed for a group photograph in the garden. There they are, those five splendid men, with barely a single tooth between them but with a wealth of Old Testament beards and sidewhiskers. In the centre sits old Richard, a smile of sheer contentment on his face. On his right is the smiling John, aged 67, and on his left, more serious but delightfully bewhiskered, sits the 65-year-old George. Standing at the back are the hale and hearty James (76) and, watch chain dangling, young Arthur, the baby of the family at 63. What a splendid brood of Norfolk lads!

Though the fields of Norfolk were well-populated with men in those earlier labour-intensive days of the agricultural industry, others sought their destiny elsewhere. It was a very patriotic era, and there were many who set off in the service of Queen and Country in the Army or Royal Navy. A quartet of such men is portrayed in a splendid photograph taken around 1910 for the Royal Norfolk Veterans' Association, the organisation which looked after the needs of ex-servicemen before the British Legion came into being in 1921.

The Pettingale brothers of Castle Rising.
Left to right: Seated — John (67), Richard (79), George (65). Standing — James (76), Arthur(63).

Four Norfolk Veterans.
Seated: W. Skoyles of Norwich (left), Private James of Hillington (right).
Standing: R. Nicholls of Yarmouth (left), Private James Olley of Blakeney (right).

Senior member of the group was W. Skoyles of Norwich, late of the Royal Navy, and the oldest Norfolk campaigner. In his nineties when the photograph was taken, he displayed a solitary medal — that of the Kaffir War of 1848. His Naval comrade amongst the quartet, R. Nicholls of Yarmouth, wore a proud clutch of decorations indicating his service in the Crimean, Turkish and Baltic Wars as well as in Chinese and New Zealand waters,

The two ex-Army men were both veterans of the Crimean and Turkish Wars of 1854. Private James, of Hillington, was a former member of the 93rd Sutherland Highlanders who had become the "Thin Red Line" at Balaclava. He also wore the medals of the Indian Mutiny of 1857 and the Afghan War, together with a long service decoration. Finally, there was the fine, upstanding figure of Private James Olley, of Blakeney, late of the 4th Light Dragoons. He must have had a tale to tell, for he was the last Norfolk survivor of the Charge of the Light Brigade.

So many men and women have trodden the fair earth of Norfolk, most of them simple folk leading simple lives, yet all with a story to tell, a memory to recount. Yet the majority, sadly, have gone to their graves taking their memories with them. There is no such thing as an ordinary life, for all encounter different experiences and our brains store up a diversity of memories. Many people are heard to say, "I often think I ought to write my life story". There is only one comment one can make in reply: "Don't just think about it — sit down and do it"; for there are, in everybody's life, memories that are unique but which, when read by others, stimulate the sights, the sounds and the scents of years gone by.

When, in 1931, B. Knyvet Wilson compiled two little books of Norfolk stories to raise funds for a local hospital charity, he saw fit to include a few memories of his own. I know of nothing else he wrote, and his little piece really contained nothing new, but it conjured up a delightful picture of yesteryear in our fair county — not to mention an insight into the author's sense of humour. He wrote:

I can stand at a gate and watch the plough turning up the rich brown-red soil for hours. Man and horses are almost hidden by the ever-wheeling grey and white cloud of attendant gulls, and the only sound is the ploughman's occasional "Wheesh, Bunny!" or "Smiler" or "Captain" or "Prince" or "Diamond" or "Boxer" (as the case may be) and the creak of the plough as it turns. My father loved it all and did not, indeed, disdain the sharp tang of the farm manure. He loved, I think, to ponder on all the good it was going to do, and would throw up his head and say, "Ah, healthy smell of muck!"

Later, about harvest time, one catches sight of a covey of partridges basking on the road or on the first stubbles. His majesty the cock pheasant — as glorious as Solomon and with nearly as many wives — lifts his gorgeous head, neck and breast in an endeavour to find out who is daring to disturb his work in the stubble. The wood pigeon too — the bane of the farmer, yet one of the most beautiful of birds. And, in the evening, dear old "Willy-owl" flops across your path in a ghost-like manner — not good for the nerves.

When I was young I loved to spend hours and hours in the blacksmith's forge. The Lansdells were ever a blacksmith family, and to watch Lou or Walter bringing down their hammers with a beautiful rhythm, while heavy molten lumps flew to all parts of the forge, was a great wonder. Then the "Piece" begins to get cold, is seized in the great nippers, thrust into the heap of coal dust, and a horny hand grasps the handle of the bellows. After a moment of roaring, sparks begin to fly from the top of the heap, out come the nippers again, and bang goes hammer on anvil. And the clink of the hammer on the anvil sometimes would mark the time. There was also the shoeing-smith, with his back to the horse's head, hoof well imprisoned between his knees and the peculiar sizzling and hot smell from the hoof as the shoe is fitted and nailed.

But the Norfolk village has lost much of its old-world family life. As I believe Lady Godiva is supposed to have said on a certain historical occasion, "Thank heaven, I am now nearing my close!"

I count myself fortunate to have lived my life in this fair county of ours. Throughout the years there has been a constant succession of people who, by their mere presence, have added colour to my existence. Most of them were simple folk leaving simple memories. It is to them that this book is dedicated.

Acknowledgements

I am grateful to those friends who have loaned me photographs to supplement my own in illustrating this book. My thanks go to Bob Briggs, Rhoda Bunn, Joan Canning, Eddie Codling, Ron Fiske, Nigel Martyn, Tony Rayna, Philip Standley, Clifford Temple, Perry Underwood, Len Vincent, Ray Woolston and Philip Yaxley.

A particular nod of appreciation goes to Ben Burgess who, having allowed me free access to his boyhood memories of Norwich Hill, accepted my invitation to write the foreword to this book with an enthusiasm which was highly infectious.

Bob Bagshaw.
Wymondham.
October 1992.